LYING BELIEFS
Stretching the boundaries on your path to enlightenment

MAURICE JOHNSON

www.nomoego.com

Published by
NoMoEgo, LLC
P.O. Box 340778
Tampa, Fl 33694-0778

(813) 546-2736

Copyright © 2016 NoMoEgo, LLC; maurice@nomoego.com
All rights reserved.

The design, content, editorial accuracy, and views expressed or implied in this work are those of the author.

No part of this publication may be reproduced, stored in a retrieval system, or transmitted in any way by any means—electronic, mechanical, photocopy, recording, or otherwise—without the prior permission of the copyright holder, except as provided by USA copyright law.

All scripture quotations, unless otherwise indicated, are taken from the Holy Bible, New International Version®, NIV®. Copyright ©1973, 1978, 1984, 2011 by Biblica, Inc.™ Used by permission of Zondervan. All rights reserved worldwide. www.zondervan.com The "NIV" and "New International Version" are trademarks registered in the United States Patent and Trademark Office by Biblica, Inc.™

Scripture references marked KJV are taken from the King James Version of the Bible.

Cover Design & Layout by DocUmeant Designs
http://www.DocUmeantDesigns.com

Third Edition

ISBN13: 978-0-692-68386-6
ISBN10: 0-692-68386-0

DEDICATION

Lying Beliefs is dedicated to my fellow human beings who *'feel'* that there is indeed some fundamental incongruence in their lives.

Based upon this subtle perception they sense that their beliefs may have been adulterated by influences designed to mislead and block the natural powers we were born with. Hence, based upon this mysterious internal feeling that comes with no explanation, these curious human beings are pursuing what may ultimately define who they are.

Contents

Dedication . . . . *iii*

Preface: My Story . . . . *vii*

Introduction: The Story of My Book . . . . *xi*

CHAPTER I: In The Beginning *1*

CHAPTER II: May I Have Your Attention Please? *13*

CHAPTER III: Is Your 'Self' The Ruler Of 'Your' Thoughts? *23*

CHAPTER IV: Are We Only Human Or Are We Only Life?. . *47*

CHAPTER V: Is Consciousness More Than Just a Mind?. . . . *61*

CHAPTER VI: What Does God Mean To You? *81*

CHAPTER VII: The Pursuit of Wholeness. *95*

CHAPTER VIII: God's Immortal Soul (Sol) *119*

CHAPTER IX: Our Heart's Sole (Sol) Purpose *159*

CHAPTER X: The Man-Made Mind *179*

CHAPTER XI: The Human Avatar. *209*

CHAPTER XII: Believing Versus Knowing. *217*

CHAPTER XIII: In the End *227*

Personal Acknowledgments *237*

Internet Acknowledgements *239*

My Glossary *241*

Professional Book Reviews **249**

Pacific Book Review Interview **251**

About the Author. **263**

Next Steps **265**

PREFACE

My Story

I am a humble soul who *feels* that the true nature of God is a Universal energy, which resides within every *living Being.* However, I am not affiliated with any religion. Every *church* that I have ever visited has left me *unfulfilled.* Therefore, you may be wondering what inspired me to write such a spiritually based book without the influence of a religious background.

Well, it's called inspiration through knowing!

Despite my limited involvement with any religious doctrine, I have always had a tremendous sense of someone or *something* within me. However, I've always been told as a youngster, that the church is where you received your spiritual nourishment and where you develop a true loving relationship with God. On the contrary, I witness more hypocrites gathered in church than I encounter on the streets. And the *religious God* that I was supposedly searching for within these religious chapels never appeared to be *present.*

I will be honest; I never dwelt upon my *true calling* in life, due to my contentment and placid personality until my near-death experience due to diabetes in January of 2006. Through my survival of this condition, I was ultimately guided towards exploring— *what was my real reason for Being?*

I later learned that the husband of my wife's friend was also admitted at the same time and also with diabetic complications.

However, what made our diabetic situations different was that he actually walked into the hospital, whereas I entered via the Emergency Room, in a wheelchair, in a diabetic coma.

I had a blood glucose level exceeding 1,300 and my kidneys were shot. I was told that I would require dialysis treatment for the rest of my life—and my heart was also on its way out too! I was in the Intensive Care Unit (ICU) for five days. I felt fortunate; my wife's friend's husband, who was admitted to the hospital at the same time I was, *did not walk out.*

I later discovered he died!

I did not know how to accept this information until four years later, during a Christmas Eve family gathering at my mother-in-law's house. I had the pleasure of meeting the widow of the man who should have been in my shoes that evening.

After conversing with this lovely lady and ascertaining the details surrounding her husband's death, *it hit me!*

Based upon what appeared to be a non-life-threatening situation she never imagined that the man she entered the hospital with would never come home.

Subsequently, this made me question, **why am I still here?**

Meanwhile, as our conversation ended with a loving embrace, she whispered in my ear and said; *"Son, God has a plan for you."*

Her whisper over time got louder and I started to open my communication channel to this Universe. I would chant on a daily basis, *"Help me see what you want me to be!"* As time passed, this recital became more frequent and more *heartfelt.*

Then on February 6, 2012, I was formally introduced to *who I am.* At this amazing moment of awareness I discovered the true meaning of *Being* born again. Hence, this level of awareness resonated throughout my body in such an *electrifying* way that I cried like a *new born baby.*

Following this experience, I was enlightened with the mysterious truth as to who we all are. I, without any hesitation, picked up a pen and begin logging wisdom which was being relayed from a pristine and serene place. The purification of knowing who we are was so intense that the truth became overwhelming.

During this enlightenment, everything became completely transparent. When we are born into this world, we arrive as *Divine Human Beings.* Then something strips us of our divinity. We become tainted and are left to live our lives in the broken *form, of being only human* versus living *'Wholly'* as prosperous human <u>Beings</u>.

Hence, our divine purpose, our real reason for *Being* is stolen; leaving us struggling with the following *self-addressed* question—*who do you think you are?*

Humanity struggles religiously with the validity of what we *think* versus what we *feel.* In other words, in this ring of life, the *Title Fight* is between what our man-made paradigms want us to *believe is true,* versus *what our Universal nature makes us feel is right.* This constant combat of emotions does not cease until we finally awaken to the reality of knowing; that what we think is true about our *'selves'* is indeed a *man-made lie!*

INTRODUCTION

The Story of My Book

Lying Beliefs is a creative non-fiction documentary designed to capture your attention and intrigue you by way of witty and imaginative analogies. Although some of the analogies maybe playful and lighthearted, the deliberate goal of this written dialogue is to grasp your awareness and plunge it deep into the vast sea of the human unknown and have you emerge with a clearer *sense* of what better defines you.

The primary purpose of this book is to take a stab at poking holes through the man-made darkness that currently occupies our subconscious mind. During this challenging process, I hope to expose your man-made paradigm enough to have the *light shine through* in order to *reveal the true you.*

Although the message communicated within *Lying Beliefs* is well beneath the surface of common thought, the information is provided in a rational tone. However, in order to *feel* the depth of the material provided you must dive in *heart* first instead of head first.

- *Lying Beliefs* addresses the *undiscovered, conscious mind.*

- *Lying Beliefs* marries the Christian religion with science, and explains how *this Universe's Sun or **El Sol** represents the **light** that defines the soul of every living being.*

- *Lying Beliefs* theoretically unveils how *oxygen* is nothing more than a linguistic term that characterizes our *consciousness*.

Lying Beliefs provides the reader with animated analogies of how our subconscious mind has freed us from our own *free will*, and unbeknownst to us, how we human beings have become *willing* servants to the *man-made beliefs* that *lie deep* within our subconscious mind. Thus, we human beings on a daily basis are being manipulated and misguided by man-made concepts that devour our divine power of love.

Therefore, if you are a human being who is seeking true freedom, then search no further. If you are willing to enter into your heart and open your *subconscious mind,* then *Lying Beliefs* will cast light upon the obscurity that bears humanity's pain and suffering. It will also introduce to your subconscious mind the *light* that illuminates who you truly are.

As a human being I have come to know that our present journey, while here on earth, is nothing more than a *conscious experience,* and every human being that is born of this sacred planet is born privileged. Therefore, no one human being is entitled to anything.

This beautiful planet that we reside on is meant to be *shared* and *not conquered.* However, based upon humanity's current man-made perception, we have all been conditioned to think otherwise.

Please know this book was not created to judge your beliefs. It was written to *shine a different light* upon our *'selves'* and our *controlling beliefs,* and to expose them for what they really are. However, after reading *Lying Beliefs,* you will be the judge and jury that determines whether or not your beliefs are *guilty* or not guilty for your *uncontrolled* behavior.

From my own *'self'*-analysis, I have come to the sound *conscious* conclusion that there are three core concepts or *beliefs* that rest within our subconscious mind that are responsible for creating what we human beings refer to as *Hell on Earth!* And they are: *our man-made concept(s) of Self, Life, and God.*

We, as humans, have grown *selfishly attached* to our self-assigned concepts of *Self, Life, and God.* This means we have been *detached* from the divine essence of love that defines our true divine nature. Thus, through this separation, we have become a very *self*-destructive species.

I know our religious beliefs may persuade us to believe that we are not born divine and this is because the universal essence of who we are was not born within our minds.

As we all know, this universe is what defines divinity; which means *divinity* is actually a synonym for *love.* Hence, we are all defined by the *divine loving energy of this Universe.*

Love is the *natural emotion* that is born in the heart of every human being. This means divinity was never instilled within our mind, because divinity has always been anchored to our heart.

In my opinion, the primary reason why we should all make a *conscious effort* to evaluate—and question—our beliefs is because we were not born with them in mind. Hence, if we did not arrive here with our beliefs in *mind*; then why do we believe they define us?

Meaning, there is not one belief that resides within our mind that constitutes as being <u>*our personal belief.*</u> Thus, every belief that we live by is a *concept that man has made us believe;* which is why I refer to our *presumed* beliefs as <u>man-made beliefs</u>, which is a reference that you will notice throughout this book.

We human beings must come to know that in regard to man's problematic version of *Self, Life, and God* our subconscious mind bares no truth, it only bares the beliefs, which we have been taught to uphold, which in turn govern our thoughts.

Therefore, true enlightenment is realizing that the sacred truth was placed deep within our heart and it was never bestowed within our subconscious mind.

Thus, the core objective of my mission is to help humanity *envision,* that beyond our conditioned man-made convictions the <u>*essence of universal love*</u> is our birthright.

In other words, as children of this divine Universe, our *'universal'* nature is the *divine power of love*. Which further means, the power of **unity** or *"one love"* can only be achieved through acknowledging that the divine nature of who we are is indeed **uni**versal.

Therefore, every *man-made concept* that we allow to redefine us, in reality *conceals the real **concept**ion* of who we are.

Hence, the 'truth' we human beings seek—'lies' beyond our man-made beliefs.

I

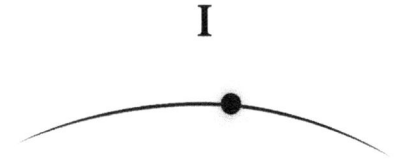

In The Beginning

Did you know in the beginning, every human being is born pure in mind, pure in body, and pure in soul?

Pure in Mind means in the beginning our subconscious mind is pure. Considering, our subconscious mind has yet to be tarnished by man-made concepts. However, the moment our subconscious mind embraces man's *belittling* notions of *Self, Life, and God* our subconscious mind becomes tainted. And once our thoughts proceed to dwell upon these *depreciating* assumptions our thoughts are converted into sinful feelings, which is why we are all said to be born sinners.

Pure in Body means our human form, at birth, is filled with the *divine* essence of *love*. However, after years of having relentless thoughts of *fear* and *worry* our human form becomes weak and weary.

Pure in Soul means since we all share the spiritual nature of this universe we will always be deemed as pure in soul or pure in spirit.

I state the above to say that shortly after the pure essence of who we are is introduced to Mother Earth, something dreadful begins to take place. A mental virus begins to establish itself within the psyche of our subconscious mind through a plethora of questionable influences, which then proceed to erase any real idea of who we are.

Chapter I

This questionable information begins to affect our subconscious mind and eventually gives birth to *beliefs* that *religiously lie* to us.

These *lying beliefs* are similar to a body snatcher because they suck the life out of our human forms and begin to take *full* control of our lives. We are transformed into human zombies; which means we are deprived of our *controlled consciousness* and *true self-awareness,* only able to respond to our surrounding stimuli.

Question: Have you ever heard the expression "The mind is a terrible thing to waste?" Do you know what the premise is behind this statement?

Well, in my opinion it means it is a terrible thing to pollute our subconscious mind with *'wasteful'* thoughts considering the end result is usually *garbage in, garbage out.*

Thus, *Lying Beliefs* has been written to question and test our paradigms to the fullest. The information within this book has been orchestrated to closely examine what we believe in. However, be warned, this book is going to push the level of your current thinking to its utmost limit.

Now, with this being said, are you ready to question the *man-made concept* of who you think you are?

<u>Alright, let the interrogation begin!</u>

First and foremost, do you believe that the majority of our beliefs are based upon a vast amount of information that should be questioned? Do you recognize that our potential is stifled because of the attention that we grant to our beliefs?

Do you know that our beliefs are direct results of our thoughts? Do you know it is only our beliefs that weaken us human beings?

Finally, do you know it is only our beliefs that lurk within our subconscious mind that create our fears and worries?

Well, if you believe that *fear* is a side effect of our beliefs then please ask your '*self*' the following crucial question: If fear completely contradicts my best interest then why do I elect to accept an emotion that is not in my sincerest interest?

As they say, "There is nothing to fear, except fear itself." So, do we fear our beliefs because what we fear seems real?

<u>Well if so, here is why:</u>

Although the majority of our beliefs are suspicious, it is simply the way they make us feel that makes us believe that they are real.

This is how it works. Depending on how intense we feel about a certain belief, the outcome of this feeling will determine the reality of our belief. The more we accept a belief as being true, the more likely we will feel that our belief is surely valid. Hence, the more powerful our belief is, the more potent our feeling will be towards thinking that our belief is indeed bona fide.

Some spiritual gurus may say that our beliefs are illusions. Even though most of our beliefs are contrived, the truth of the matter is whether they are distorted or not, they still form our reality. The unfortunate moral to this sad story is that because we live our entire lives relying on man-made beliefs, these beliefs have led us astray. Since we have allowed man's questionable beliefs to misguide us, we have in turn collectively created a reality that resembles a *lost world*.

Although the bulk of our beliefs may be delusional, each belief has been leveraged to construct this biased world that we live in. What we subjectively see is an imaginary portrait that has been painted by our tainted beliefs and which portrays our troublesome reality. In other words, each hallucinatory manifestation of a disturbing belief is a byproduct of our tarnished imagination.

Have you ever heard the following expression "You see and hear what you want?"

Chapter I

Well, whether we realize this or not, this is *not* simply a figure of speech, it is actually a bona fide reality. Realize that it is only our *beliefs* that determine our perception. Therefore, what we see and hear are indeed limited by what we believe.

<u>*Here is an example of what I mean*</u>.

Let's say that you have come to the conclusion that your significant other is guilty of something; therefore you begin to seek for clues that will validate your theory.

And Walla!

You believe you have finally discovered the evidence that will confirm your suspicion. When in truth, what you *thought* was bona fide evidence, was in reality irrelevant. It was only your *subconscious perception* that made you believe that your significant other was guilty of something that was in fact a manifestation of a hallucination. This allowed you to see and hear what you suspected in order to satisfy your subconscious suspicion.

In light of the above example, please realize that an *incongruent emotion* that we receive from our man-made paradigm is drastically different from a *congruent feeling* of *internal intuition*.

Our thoughts, whether good or bad, are the *seeds* that are *planted* within the *soil* of our subconscious mind which ultimately *blossoms* our reality.

Will we ever become Heavenly human beings?

We will never become *Heavenly* human beings until we recognize our *divinity*. In other words, we will never experience *"Heaven on Earth"* until we realize that we are all *born divine* at birth. Therefore, if we continue to fail at shifting our awareness upon the essence that truly defines us, then we will die containing an invaluable hidden secret.

Okay, I have a valuable question to ask you. Do you realize there is no true gratification in material wealth, only pacification?

We human beings need to discern that there is no one thing that is materially created that will ever fulfill our core needs. Hence, true fulfillment is solely our responsibility. Regardless of our material achievements in life we will forever feel that something utterly important is missing—until we discover what defines us.

<u>Let's use the following as an example</u>:

Okay, let's say that we have accomplished everything our ego has set forth for us to achieve; we have completely satisfied our ego's bidding. Let's also say we have a billion dollar bank account and we have acquired more material items than we know what to do with. Most people envy us solely based upon our material worth. Although we have fulfilled all of our ego's requests and wants we sense that there is still something substantial missing from our life. However, we can't quite place our finger on it.

Now as we all know, once our Earthly experience comes to an end, our billions are worthless and every single material possession we owned is meaningless. In the grand scheme of things, it never mattered anyway since this man-made wealth we sacrificed our life for, never really provided our *genuine essence* with any *real value*.

So, after it is all said and done, regardless how *'materially'* rich we were, if we never discover who we truly are, then we will unfortunately die in the same manner in which we lived—broke. In other words, if we allow our material achievements to become our perception of who we are, then we will always be spiritually bankrupt.

In order to harness our ego we must refrain from allowing our occupation or our material possessions to exemplify who we are. If we allow these *shallow* expressions of self-representation to *fully* define us then the very moment these self-identified notions no longer exist our very own existence suddenly becomes *empty.*

Once we understand and embrace the true astonishing, hidden treasure that resides within our human form we will begin to refurbish our self-worth and become overflowing with credit-worthiness. Therefore, please do not envy another man's material riches, because a man's material wealth may mean that he is poor in spirit. And if a man is unaware of his divine essence then he suffers from a greater poverty.

The true value of any human being can only be measured by the *Estate* of his or her spirituality.

Question: Do you know that we are all 'slaves' to the beliefs that 'master' our subconscious mind?

We human beings are slaves to our man-made sense of self. We are slaves to man's concept of life, and we are slaves to man's *self-serving* religion(s).

So in a nutshell, we are *servants* to our *man-made* or *Lying Beliefs!* And the only reason we continue to invite lying beliefs into our lives, is because our subconscious mind has never been introduced to the *truth!*

Here's the ultimate question: How do we expect to achieve what our true heart's desire without being conscious of who we truly are?

The real reason we all live a *subconscious life* is because we tend to lend our awareness to the beliefs that live within our subconscious mind. Once our beliefs capture our attention we are held as prisoners within the walls of our own subconscious minds. This means we are no longer free to appreciate the glory of *authentic* life, because we are now captivated by a *synthetic* reality.

Let me ask you a question: Do you ever feel like you are only existing through life, rather than living? In other words do

you ever feel like there is something essentially missing from your life?

If so, you are not alone. Most of humanity needs to break free of this hypnotic state of existing and try to focus on genuine living through becoming more aware of an essence that supersedes who we think we are.

See, we are only privy to a pseudo sense of who we are and this incomplete description is captured through our human faculties of sight and sound. These two key physical senses are primary in developing our man-made sense of self.

Humanity, more often than not, seems to gravitate towards believing in man's questionable hearsay and taxing perception of life without any confirmation of this debatable information that is being administered to us through our subconscious mind. Thus, this *absent awareness* towards living in the moment is what begins to develop our troublesome paradigms and why we human beings *incoherently struggle* through life.

What I find scary is the fact that we tend to lean on our paradigms for truth. Unfortunately, these man-made concepts that occupy our paradigms are often found to be inaccurate and misleading.

<u>*Here is an example of what I mean*</u>:

If we are conditioned to believe that something ambiguous is bona fide and we maintain this particular illusion for years, this misconception—per our misguided awareness—will be considered as gospel. No matter what anyone says, their opinion will not sway our man-made belief.

Thus, if we are devoted to man's religious concept(s) of Jesus, Allah, Buddha, Jehovah, etc., it's highly unlikely that anyone will be able to alter the love that we have formed for our elected God(s).

Therefore, please realize the nature of any *man-made concept* will not reveal itself until we make a *controlled conscious* effort to recognize the man-made belief for what it is.

Do you know we are not who we "think" we are?

Have you ever wondered if we are all born 'whole' as human beings; then when did we become 'divided' as human races?

Our beliefs have bestowed upon us a false perception of self. And as we interact with other human beings we provide each other with a *fake form* of identification. Perhaps this is why we have been arrested by our subconscious minds.

This man-made perception of self is what gave birth to what we now call the human race. In truth, we are not part of a human race; we are all divine human beings. Nonetheless, our beliefs have separated us based upon a difference in human form and we have all been grouped accordingly.

Okay, now that we have all been physically divided it's off to the *races* and may the most *subconsciously* driven race win. See, as this so called human race races on, our ego will be our coach as well as our cheerleader. And whichever race is in the lead, their egos will keep their human forms fueled and driven to win.

With all this being said, please note life was not created to be played; it was designed to be *playful*. Therefore, whichever member of this so called human race happens to be the first to cross this man-made finish line; it will definitely be the end.

Thus, in reality, there are no true winners in this man-made game that we call *life,* since man's version of life is not about *living*, considering it's all about *having*. See, most of humanity is focused on the *material* things in life versus simply being a part of life. Therefore, as a whole, we all lose because there will always be a battle between the *"haves and have-nots."* This means the more material that you possess; the more possessed the less fortunate will be to take what you have.

All analogies aside, it's sad how we are all being ruled by our man-made paradigms. In essence we are all the same because we are all created in the *divine energy* of this Universe. Which means it is only our *beliefs* that make us all appear to be substantially different.

What I find interesting is how we cherish beliefs that have been passed down to us from our family and society as being our very own beliefs. Our convictions that we defend, for the most part, are cultural concepts that we have been conditioned to believe are true. We only think our beliefs are valid because everyone else appears to share these same *unconfirmed* concepts.

The beliefs that we guard with all our heart, are really not our beliefs, they are nothing more than family heirlooms that have been handed down and implanted within our subconscious minds. So, in theory it should be these *family beliefs*, which we do not question that we should be most skeptical of.

In a nutshell, it is our conditioned cultural beliefs that we individually uphold that separates us. Hence, we humans are religiously being brainwashed on a daily basis. My personal perception of brainwashing is: *The result of the damaging man-made rhetoric that has been poured into our subconscious minds from an early age has washed away any sign of our divinity.*

Does it ever cross your awareness why we human beings suffer?

Well in my opinion, we human beings as a whole suffer from having one debilitating monster commonly referred to as the *Human Ego!*

Each and every one of us has our own *tailor-made ego* which has been suited to *inappropriately* fit who we think we are. This regulating ego is responsible for our human agony. We must understand that our human frustrations are a direct result of a man-made condition that is the consequence of man-made concepts.

Since we have carelessly granted our awareness to our man-made perception of self, our man-made sense of self is now equipped to drive our human framework throughout life in a reckless manner by way of controlling our thoughts and awareness. Therefore, freedom can only be accomplished by liberating our awareness from the mental bondage of who we *subconsciously* think we are.

Do you ever struggle with being conscientious about what you are doing during any given moment?

If so, guess what— this is something that most of humanity has in common. We, as human beings, have an extreme problem with being able to control our consciousness and because we can't seem to achieve this control we have lost complete control of our *selves*. In other words, we human beings have yet to learn how to *control the state of our subconscious minds.*

There really isn't anything we *'physically'* do in the present moment that has our undivided attention. While we are cleaning, eating, bathing, etc… our thoughts are usually elsewhere.

Please understand being *subtracted* from controlled consciousness means we are being *distracted* from who we are, which *equates* to *attracting* our human suffering.

In case you didn't know, our paradigms are an exceptionally hard nut to crack.

Therefore, the core objective of *Lying Beliefs* is to make a valid attempt to penetrate this seemingly impenetrable entity. Thus, readers of this work should not be referring to the current state of their subconscious minds for validation.

If you allow your *'self'* to be accessible to receiving a loving source of refreshing information, which is not *presently* resting within your subconscious mind, then the information that is outlined in this book will at least put an *enlightening* chip in your man-made beliefs.

However, please know that my ultimate goal is not to just chip away at your paradigm because I am aiming to *shatter* it in order to help rescue *you* from your *'self'*. And please do not walk away after reading this book with another formed belief. Simply believing in what has been written is not enough.

Lying Beliefs has been created to help us personally discover the true essence of who we are and only through this encounter will this book have served its divine purpose.

Lying Beliefs also marries the Christian religion with science in order to create a Holy/*Wholly* matrimony. Through this union, the sacred secret of who we are is revealed.

Therefore as an important *side note,* please note that the mention of any religious dogma within this book has not been intended to offend or upset anyone. It has been written to reveal the truth about the concept of religion in general, as well as, to cast a *shining new light* upon an ancient message—which to this day still appears to be *cloudy.*

Before we take a *deep* dive into *Lying Beliefs*, I just want to say as a fellow human being that I feel it is my personal responsibility to share with humanity what I have experienced. Sharing with our fellow humans what we have encountered during our Earthly explorations is one of the key purposes in life.

My *soul* goal is to provide humanity with an enlightening compass that will show the way to reveal who we are. Once our true identity is no longer concealed; only then will our *true light* be revealed.

Whether humanity knows this or not; we are all in *solitary* confinement within our own subconscious mind and our ego is the controlling warden.

Chapter I

Therefore, my intention is to shift humanity's awareness towards the sacred truth that defines us all. This will allow an escape from this mental prison so that we do not live a *life sentence* as a fugitive within a *self-destructive* Hell Hole.

II

May I Have Your Attention Please?

<u>May I have your attention please?</u>

I wonder if we grasp the significance of this solicitation. I wonder if we truly comprehend the magnitude of such a request.

Do you know relinquishing our attention to someone or to something means everything? Do you know if our attention is placed in the wrong hands, this could be devastating to our life? Do you know if we do not manage our attention, someone else will? Do you know that every time we pay attention there may be a price to pay?

In the grand scheme of our reality our attention is all we have. Therefore, it is vital to our reality that we are cognizant of where our attention lives. With this being said, please take time out of your busy schedule and do you (and I do really mean *you* and not your '*self*' a favor, and spy on where *your* attention dwells.

I ask that you follow your attention within the parameters of your subconscious mind and notice where it spends most of its time and then analyze how you feel.

Whether you recognize this or not, *you* are what is considered to be *your attention*. This means in reality that you need to investigate where **'you'** spend the most of your time.

Please understand that where our attention lives determines where we live, regardless of where our human form resides. Where our attention travels eventually outlines the road map of our life's journey.

Every human being should learn how to distribute their attention wisely, because every single day someone or something is grasping for it. On a daily basis we have family members, friends, acquaintances, advertisements, etc., constantly demanding our attention. And once our attention is given, the astonishing outcome is simply a *feeling*. And wouldn't you agree what we feel means everything to us?

Feelings are one of the most essential things that we humans all have in common, yet we do not share a common interest in how we feel. We all struggle with the complexity of our feelings, but one thing is for sure—we are all in pursuit of the same *universal* feeling.

All the things we work towards to achieve and accomplish in life are performed to spark a specific feeling. Our lives are complex interactions of *cause and effect*. The cause of our vested hard work and our drive towards obtaining material goals is done to produce an effective feeling.

In other words, what *cause* us to do certain things in our lives are usually motivations to stimulate feelings that cast the *effects of immeasurable joy*.

So, with this being said; do you know our feelings are the foundation to our reality?

Now in regards to our feelings being the foundation to our reality let's use the definition of life as an example. The meaning of life is defined by one thing and one thing only—how life makes us *feel*.

I feel that it is safe to say, that a vast majority of what we believe in is indeed questionable. And as I mentioned *"In The Beginning"*, some Spiritual Teachers may even say our beliefs are an illusion. However, despite how indefinite or illusive our beliefs are, there is one thing that goes without question. That is that, the result of our beliefs, whether imaginary or not, definitely creates a *feeling* that seems *very real.* The irony is, although our beliefs may feel real, this doesn't necessarily mean that they actually are real. Whether we realize this or not, our beliefs are not defined by *truth and certainty.*

Whatever we choose to believe in is designed to form our *personal **reality** by creating a feeling that honors our beliefs.* In other words, our beliefs are only responsible for manifesting a *feeling* that reinforces our *reality.*

Beyond what we have been conditioned to believe, we are all one and we all share in the same divine nature; hence we are all *born to feel and experience the same common emotion* and that is *love;* which I will expand upon in a later chapter. However for now, let's get back to what we believe in, or in other words, what we *feel* is real.

As it stands now we may believe or feel that we are different from other human beings for one reason or another. And with this being said, it seems that the top two reasons associated with these beliefs are related to a difference in physical appearance and a variance in geographic culture. Thus, if our attention remains focused on what *physically contains* us; then it will be virtually impossible to ever see another human being as we see ourselves.

Do you know what the contrast is between oneness and selfishness?

The feelings of love and peace can only be cultivated through the discovery of divine *oneness.* However, until the idea of unity takes place and becomes a permanent landscape within our subconscious mind we will continue to breed hate and separation via the attention we bestow upon our man-made *selfishness.*

Chapter II

We must acknowledge that peace can only be achieved through oneness. True peace and unity is accomplished through knowing that a piece of you indeed lives within all forms of life and vice versa. Through this unified perception of oneness human beings tend to see all forms of life as being synonymous. Though, through the split perspective of selfishness, we perceive all forms of life as a contradiction to what we stand for.

Therefore, our *self-centered* beliefs tend to generate disharmony; not only towards other human beings, but also within our '*self*'.

Speaking of our 'self'; do you know that there's a monumental difference between 'you' and your 'self'?

Some spiritual individuals tend to say that in order to become enlightened, we need to make a mental connection with our *higher self.* However, during my quest for the truth I simply preferred to leave my *elevated self* completely out of the equation of enlightenment.

In my opinion, it is my '*self*' that is the primary culprit in all my problems. Therefore, success in obtaining true enlightenment can only be achieved by simply knowing *who I am.* I have already spent the vast majority of my life becoming very well acquainted with my '*self*' and I must say at times my '*self*' can be very annoying. From my perspective it is my '*self*' that is the root from which stems my **self**ishness.

I have come to realize that my '*self*' was born shortly after 'I' arrived here on this beautiful planet. Hence, it was the rise of my man-made '*self*' that laid the *soul of who I am* down to rest.

Understand that the energy that *we* exude to protect our '*self*' is what grants our '*self*' life. In other words, our '*self*' was not created to protect *us,* considering it was formulated to defend the man-made concept of it'*self*'.

What I find to be intriguing is the nature that truly defines me is *untouchable*, yet stable with enormous substance and energy that bears no alteration. Hence, it is unlike my *'self'*, which is unruly, forever changing, and *selfishly* requires my *undivided attention.*

<u>With this being stated, you may frequently ask your *'self'* the following question: Who Am I?</u>

Unfortunately this is a question that your *'self'* will never be equipped to answer. Quite frankly, this is an answer that your *'self'* works day and night to keep from you. Therefore, it is up to **you** to make this determination on behalf of your *'self'*.

Do you know that our 'self' controls our thoughts? Do you know that our 'self' rules our reality? Did you know that our 'self' and our 'ego' are one in the same?

Did you know that our 'self' is a monster that we unknowingly created? In other words, do you realize that our 'ego' is a 'self' controlling monster?

In order for us to live a peaceful and happy life; our *'selves'* simply must go. And since we help create this man-made monster, it is up to us to destroy it, or at least tame it.

<u>Question: do any of the following statements sound familiar?</u>

You need to gain more *self*-control! *You* need to get a hold of your *'self'*! Based on these statements alone it should be easy to envision that *you* and your *self* can't possibly be one in the same.

These statements speak volumes in regards to the distinct difference between *you* and your *'self'*. However, it is up to **you** to make this very important distinction to help *you* to overcome this self-made monster you unknowingly created.

The irony is, our *'self'* does not need to be saved, considering our *'self'* is free doing what it wants. Which means our life's mission is to actually save *who we are* from our *'self'*. And despite what we have been taught to believe, this is a rescue mission that is solely our responsibility.

The truth is *we* cannot share the same reality with our *'self'*. This means only one of us can exist. Until we recognize the authenticity of who we are, our *selfish ego* will continue to supervise our thoughts and rule our reality.

The only way we will ever be able to gain complete control of our lives is through recognizing that *we* and our *'self'* are not one in the same. By way of this understanding, we will then be able to sever the relationship that we have formed with our ego, and this will in turn free us from our mental hell cell.

Now in order to accomplish this seemingly impossible feat, as Jesus said, *your 'self' must die!*

Now you are probably scratching your head saying, well, how do I destroy my *'self'*, without eliminating *who I am*? And quite frankly this is a valid inquiry; considering we will never lay our *'self'* down to rest, until we first discover what genuinely defines us.

Note: this discovery will be revealed in a later chapter.

However, as Jesus said, in order for *you* to be *"born again"* your *'self'* must die. In other words, the man-made *lie* that we believe defines us must *die*.

Do you have any idea why most of humanity is parading through life sporting a pseudo self-image?

Well, it's because our subconscious mind is only equipped to provide us with an image that suits our beliefs, and because we believe that our racial labels are status quo. Our subconscious minds can only provide us with an identity that we think is suitable.

<u>*For an example*</u>:

We human beings believe that it is normal to act only as we appear, whether that is *White, Black, Hispanic, Asian, etc.,* and of course the list of what appears to be normal is endless. Humanity needs to bring an immediate end to this man-made list of what appears to be status quo.

Have you ever attempted to grant your attention to who 'you' are? And when I say who 'you' are please know once again that I am not referring to your 'self'.

We often lend our attention to others, as well as to our *'selves'*. However, we pay no attention to who we are; and yet, who we are yearns for its *own* attention every day. As long as our-*selves* continue to possess our attention, we will never become aware of who we really are.

I must say that I am fortunate to have been formally introduced to who I am. Through this introduction, I have come to know that I am solely a conscious Being. Without the energy of my consciousness, my subconscious mind would not be able to shape my physical reality. And as a conscious Being, I am the divine energy that neither I, nor anyone else for that matter will ever be able to eyewitness; yet I *feel and sense* every aspect of my *Being*. Thus, I respect and understand that the *man-made development* of our individual paradigms makes us struggle with the idea that we are intangible conscious Beings.

I know it's perplexing to believe that the true definition of who we are is actually an intangible energy that cannot be physically detected. I know it seems futile to be able to wrap our awareness around something that we cannot wrap our arms around. In other words, I know that we are conditioned to believe: *how can I be what I do not see?*

Chapter II

However, when we become tired of being held captive by our limiting beliefs, we will then find that there is nothing more than the essential energy of *'Being'* conscious that defines us all.

We human beings live under the notion that we must believe in something, which means if we do not believe or stand for something then we are subject to fall for anything. The irony is, if you *know nothing*, then you are more apt to *believe anything.*

See, our beliefs are formulated through a lack of knowing. Thus, we tend to believe in whatever seems to be generally acceptable or popular, all because we know no better. And when I say we know no better, I am simply referring to the fact that we have no clue as to what really defines us. Once we interject who we are into our subconscious minds, this level of knowing will then shatter our man-made beliefs.

These divisive beliefs that we hold dear to our hearts can only be dissolved through the enlightenment of knowing what *truly* defines us. And as they say, *"Only the truth can set you free."* In other words, the only way we will ever transform into better human beings, is through knowing what better defines us.

The main reason we can't seem to discover who we are is because our attention is constantly being distracted by our *'self' images.* See, the irony is; a blind man is more apt to envision the truth, simply because he is not *blinded* by what he *physically* sees.

Please understand the purpose of what I speak of is not an attempt to convince anyone that all man-made concepts are bad ideas and therefore should be banished.

What I am trying to convey is that the awful misconception of who we think we are needs to be buried, so that the *true spirit* of who we are can rise and shine. And by way of this resurrection, we will then know which man-made conceptions require restoration.

Hey, can you keep a secret?

Well, I am usually pretty good about keeping secrets. However, this one I can't contain anymore; considering it is eating away at my core.

Our ego has a BIG SECRET that it does not want us to know. See, the more attention we give it, the more it grows.

As long as you believe what your ego tells you is true; the more 'will power' your ego will have over you.

As long as we are the star performers in our man-made reality show, we will never envision the 'light' that makes us glow.

When we plug into the electrifying fact that the soul is me; this is when our egos will have no choice but to set us free.

See, the real reason we are still trapped within the mental cell of our subconscious mind is because our ego has convinced us that life in the light of the present moment is boring. So, we have been led into the darkness instead.

However, despite what our egos have persuaded us to believe, the present moment is far from boredom; it is actually freedom. Therefore, as it is commonly said; if you want real freedom, then you must "get out of your head!"

We human beings must face the fact that we spend the bulk of our lives inside of our heads. And despite what we may believe, the attention that we *uncontrollably* lend to the man-made mayhem that occupies our subconscious mind is not normal.

Thus, as it relates to the Universal lifeline of all other living species; we human beings, based upon our behavior, are the most *abnormal* species ever to exist.

III

Is Your 'Self' The Ruler Of 'Your' Thoughts?

We are often asked the following questions: *How do we feel about our 'self' or what do we think of our 'self'?*

However, the real concern should be: *How does our 'self' make us 'think' and feel about who we are?*

Here's an example of how our 'self' is truly the ruler of 'our' thoughts:

We may believe that **we** are responsible for talking our *'selves'* out of what we want out of life; to the contrary, it is only our man-made *'self'* that is liable for deterring **us** from our heart-felt desires.

See, we human beings have no *'self'* control because our *selves* are in total control of our thoughts, or in better words, *in complete control of our lives*. And because our *selves* are so predominant, most of humanity doesn't like to be alone with them *'selves'*, and in fact for the most part, we actually *fear our 'selves'*.

Chapter III

The influence of 'thought' is powerful. Do you know we human beings are the only living species equipped to 'think' in order to shape our reality?

In other words, as unique Beings of this Universe, our thoughts are what drives and steers us towards our destination in life. So I ask you, what do you 'think' you are destined for?

<u>Before you address your life's journey; allow me to ask you, do you know what our thoughts are made of?</u>

Thoughts are made of *electromagnetic energy*. This electromagnetic energy is generated by the so-called *conscious mind* which is responsible for those things we do knowingly to produce thoughts. Some individuals believe consciousness and thought are what distinguishes human beings from other animals.

Well in my opinion, to inquire if other living species are conscious really shouldn't even be up for debate. It is utterly absurd to think otherwise. If we pay close attention to our household pet(s) we will notice that they exude more awareness than we do.

Now, as it relates to whether or not other living life forms *think*, well this is a valid question. I know our level of thinking is beyond that of other animals. However, I do feel every living species thinks on an instinctive level rather than on a *rational* level. *I will expand upon this later in this chapter.*

Nonetheless, do you know our thoughts, along with the assistance of our subconscious mind, are responsible for establishing our reality? Do you know that our thoughts are responsible for generating either negative or positive energy within our body?

In other words, did you know what we feel is a direct result of what we think? Did you know there is nothing outside of our thoughts that define who we think we are? Did you know there is nothing more valuable or invaluable than our thoughts?

Is Your 'Self' The Ruler Of 'Your' Thoughts?

Every wakening moment we are consumed by our thoughts and there is nothing that is more essential to the manifestation of our reality than the *intangible energy* of our thoughts. So with this being said, I ask you two very meaningful questions:

1. Who do you think you are?

2. What is your personal definition of life?

Now, if I had to gamble, I would have say that the only place you have searched for an answer to these two haunting inquiries was within the confines of your subconscious mind where everything we think upon lives.

Our subconscious mind is where every conscious experience we have deemed to be valid is stored. Every man-made *concept, theory, idea, and belief* that we have been convinced that it is of value is hoarded within this central location for safe keeping.

Our subconscious mind is where our attention *automatically* travels to pursue answers about who we are. Our attention also taps into our subconscious mind for instructions on how we should live our lives.

In other words, our subconscious mind is the only domain that we venture into for our *'self'* identity, as well as, for our *selfish* man-made version of life.

We also use our subconscious minds to determine how we perceive other human beings, and depending on what we may have been conditioned to believe, this man-made perception could be destructive thoughts of hate.

<u>With all this said; do you ever think to question your man-made data?</u>

Chapter III

I would have to say that the majority of us really do not give our paradigms a *second thought*; yet we spend a *lifetime* defending them.

<u>*Why is this?*</u>

<u>*Why do we spend an enormous amount of energy securing what could be pointless?*</u>

Well, the answer is quite simple. We have been conditioned to believe that the information which formulates our man-made paradigm is indeed what defines us. And because we know no better, we fight to maintain our beliefs.

Did you know that every belief is a man-made concept? Therefore, with this being asked couldn't there be tremendous room for error? What if our primary beliefs were actually false? What if you finally discovered who you truly are; would you still be willing to safeguard a man-made belief?

In other words, would you be willing to die for a man-made lie?

Well, I am going to assume the answer to this inquiry is NO! And based upon my assumption; don't you think we should explore the possibility that there may be something more substantial to who we are than what we have been conditioned to believe?

However, most of us human beings believe if this something that is supposedly more substantial is *intangible*; then how can it be real?

Most of humanity thinks the pursuit for the unknown or the quest for something that we cannot physically see is a ludicrous and impossible task. Therefore, we are willing to accept life for what it is and will continue to believe that there is no hope for this world that we currently live in.

Hence, we humans will proceed to believe that the faith that we have invested in our chosen religions will one day pay off and save us from this place we call Hell. However, the reality is, this beautiful planet which we have inherited is far from Hell, it is actually *"Heaven on Earth."*

See, what we human beings fail to realize is that we have collectively created this Hell on Earth, based upon our man-made concepts of *Self, God, and our distorted perspective of what we think life is.* Because our core beliefs make us believe that we are different from one another we tend to act in accordance with these disruptive man-made perceptions. And as it relates to our man-made sense of self, we human beings have been trained to believe that our physical appearance is what defines us and makes us different from one another. Based upon our unique physical appearances, we are all born into a racial concept that corresponds with who we think we should be.

Thus, we are taught that we should act and behave according to the way we look. And this distorted belief of who we think we are is recycled from generation to generation. And since we feel an *obligation* to uphold these misconceived concepts, we are *collectively* responsible for creating our own *man-made Hell on Earth*.

What I find fascinating is since we know no better, we choose to believe that there is a mysterious monster called a *Devil* that is responsible for creating our misfortune. In reality it is only our *beliefs that generate these evil thoughts* that result in our seemingly sinful nature. In other words, the concept of a Devil lives only within the intricate details of our beliefs.

If we do not eventually snap out of this *man-made hell spell* and take *conscious charge* of our own lives, we will continue to allow questionable concepts to control our thinking, which will in turn continue to promote our *devilish behavior.*

I am willing to bet that there isn't a human being alive that believes deep down inside that this is the way life should be. Yet, we still choose to focus on what we think makes us different, versus trying to detect what makes us all the same. Hence, the only way we will ever make a difference on this planet, is through realizing that beneath the surface of what we think; we all share the same *divine* nature.

The reality is we are all created to make a difference. However, it is only our paradigms that make us believe that we are all created to be different.

We human beings will always be defiant, as long as we remain compliant with our man-made sense of self.

<u>*Did you know our subconscious mind is where our ego resides? Heck, not only resides, but Governs?*</u>

Our ego is what actually defines our *'self'*. Whether we recognize this or not, our ego is a subconscious illusion of *who we think we are*.

In other words, our ego represents a *man-made belief* that we have accepted as being our real representative, simply because we have *no real idea* what really defines us.

Do you know we spend the majority of our life thinking about suspicious man-made data stored within our subconscious minds?

Did you know that the energy from our thoughts stems from our consciousness? In other words, whether a thought is coherent or incoherent, it is still a byproduct of our conscious energy.

Do you know our subconscious mind processes every thought that we feed to our man-made paradigm and then proceeds to formulate our reality?

So, what if the information that our subconscious mind develops and supplies to us is indeed invalid and detrimental to our overall well-being?

Well guess what? The reality is, our subconscious mind does not decipher what could be harmful to us or not. Our subconscious mind was created to obey our every command *by responding to every thought it receives*. So in reality, our subconscious mind only has our best interest in mind. Whatever we deem to be interesting, our subconscious mind will presume that we have bestowed upon it a *thoughtful* request.

Unfortunately, since we have yet to discover who we are, we have in turn failed to *consciously* think for our *'selves'*. Therefore, we unknowingly rely on our paradigms to think for us.

And although our paradigms are not directly responsible for producing our thoughts, they are indeed the *conductors* of our thinking. Which means the more *uncontrolled* attention we surrender to the man-made information stored within our subconscious mind; the more bandwidth we give to our *egos* to become the maestros of our lives.

<u>*Do you know how self-destructive our thoughts can be? If not here's an example*</u>:

Unfortunately, there are human beings on this planet who believe they are inferior to other human beings.

<u>*So, let's first address this issue*</u>:

My question regarding this issue is what would make a human being hate another human being in such a manner that their life's mission was designed to prevent another human being from prospering? Well, I would have to presume that a behavior of this magnitude has less to do with what they think about another human being and more with what they *think* about them *'selves'*.

Now let's speak to those individuals who do believe in this *self-destructive* concept that they are subordinate to another human being. But, first let's understand that we will never hear these human beings verbally admit to having an inferior complex. And quite frankly, their verbal declaration is not necessary. Because the reality is what we say for the most part is insignificant since what we *think* about most speaks for itself.

However, these individuals who do suffer from an inferiority complex tend to oblige this man-made idea of being a lesser human being. Thus, they proceed to conduct themselves in a compliant manner, by displaying a demeanor that is congruent with inadequacy.

The sad moral of this story is that these individuals, through their negative man-made programming, have no value for their lives or for the lives of other human beings that resemble their physical appearance. Hence, these beings tend to see themselves as being worthless. Therefore, they are more apt to disrespect and devalue their lives, as well as, the lives of other human beings that reflect their own personal image.

This misguided perception of self is what depletes a human being's life. And if you happen to be an individual who suffers from this mental misconception then please know there is a more extraordinary 'you' that is awaiting your attention.

Therefore, you need to shift your awareness from being *'self'* conscious to being more conscious of *you*. And please know, when you find out who you really are and *lose your 'self'* you will gain so much more.

When we buy into the *self-destructive* notion that we are inferior to another human being, we are more apt to inflict harm upon our *'self'* and also upon those who mirror our *'self'* imposed image.

Did you know approximately ninety-five percent of our behavior is automatic?

Which means for the most part we have no say in what we do. Just as any physically learned repetitive process eventually becomes automatic, our behavior shares the same robotic pattern.

Please allow me to explain:

When we first learn how to drive a car or ride a bike our attention is on full throttle. This means we are conscious of every action that is needed in order to master the required techniques at hand. And by way of us repeating certain processes over-and-over again, we ultimately develop all the appropriate skills necessary to effectively operate our vehicles.

Once we have perfected the required processes, something interesting happens. Our consciousness is no longer needed. Our subconscious mind has registered all the actions we have consciously put forth towards accomplishing our goal by storing each conscious decision.

So, we have now been freed from having to consciously think about the routine actions of how to drive a car or ride a bike ever again. Our subconscious mind has now taken this tedious responsibility off our hands.

Therefore, we are now 'free' to think about something else. Our subconscious mind will now, *automatically* perform each learned task for us.

For example:

As we are physically positioned behind the wheel of our automobile, our subconscious mind is *automatically* assisting our human form with the operation and control of our vehicle.

However, *we* on the other hand, via the detour *our attention* has taken to avoid the present moment, are most likely cruising through a troublesome area within our subconscious mind, *unaware* of the reality of life, which during this present moment is currently passing us by.

Now as I mentioned a moment ago, the same rule applies to our behavior. See, as young conscious beings we are conditioned to believe in a conglomeration of things. Every belief that we hold dear to our heart is a direct byproduct of this repetitive conditioning. It is those we love and trust that perpetuate our beliefs and are responsible for constructing and customizing our paradigms.

Almost every man-made belief that we are loyal to is indeed *learned.* And as we frequently accept certain taught beliefs as being true, this continuous brainwashing begins to wash away any true sense of who we are.

These concerning beliefs slowly begin to penetrate and imbed themselves within the psyche of our subconscious mind which in turn erases our true identity. Furthermore, what's really disturbing is that every human being on this planet seems to be unaware that this destructive process is continuously taking place.

Any information that we are regularly taught to believe will eventually become the blueprint that will determine how we view our *'self'*, as well as, how we perceive other human beings.

<u>So with the above being said, let's address how our behavior is also driven on auto-pilot.</u>

If we have been taught over-and-over again to hate any human being who bears an appearance that conflicts with our own and our subconscious mind has been wide open towards accepting this assignment, then sooner or later this detri*mental* programming will become a part of our paradigm.

Once this disturbing belief is stored in our subconscious mind we will never have to consciously act upon this belief again, because from this day forth our obedient subconscious mind will automatically activate this belief for us.

Hence, the moment we encounter another human being that presents a conflict in physical appearance, without any conscious effort on our part, our subconscious mind will step in on our behalf and *automatically trigger* our belief of hate towards an unknowing human being or at least a feeling of dissatisfaction.

Unfortunately, each of us participates in preserving these atrocious beliefs by harboring our own adverse negative intentions. Because we all buy into this man-made concept of being different, we *reinforce* each other's adverse perception of self.

I know we battle with the idea that beyond what we see we are all the same because of our obvious physical and behavioral differences. Although, the differences we focus on are indeed irrelevant in comparison to the intangible nature that defines us. In truth, we do possess different, or as I prefer to say *unique,* personalities.

Nonetheless, even beyond our unique personalities, there lives a divine Universal energy that grants us our awareness. This divine energy that flows through my physical form is the *exact same* mystical energy that flows through your framework, as well as, through every other form of life on this planet.

The human heart does not simply pump blood throughout our veins. The heart actually transports the esoteric energy of conscious life throughout our veins. *(Note: I will elaborate upon this concept in an upcoming chapter).* Hence, we are all one with the Universal conscious energy of life which we human beings refer to as God.

In reality it's our intangible thoughts that contain the divine force of energy which determines how we *feel* about ourselves, as well as, how we view other forms of life.

It is only our beliefs, which are programmed into our psyche, that support our conflicting perspective of what we think life is. This makes us all perceive life so differently.

Therefore, in truth, it is what we don't see that creates our reality. In other words, it is the *attention* that we grant to our *beliefs* that makes us all believe we are so dissimilar. Thus, based upon our man-made reality we are more at war with our *selves*, than we are with each other. Meaning; *"We are our own worst enemy."*

Chapter III

Do you realize there is not a day that goes by when we are not completely lost in subconscious thought?

Our oblivious state of living all starts with our thoughts that are constantly being served and fed to us in a big bowl of degradation by our paradigms. And since we are unaware of the blind attention that we lend to our subconscious mind; this incoherency forces us to focus upon what we have been conditioned to believe. Depending on how fond we are of what we have been taught this will determine how much of our man-made rhetoric will be believed. This man-made propaganda that we carelessly dwell upon, will ultimately transform our thoughts into a bona fide belief whether the conviction is true or not.

Every single aspect of our lives is governed by our thoughts. So, if at any moment you are thinking how detached you feel from your life and how this lifeless sensation develops an overall deserted feeling of being lost with no real direction then this feeling is a direct result of being completely *lost in subconscious thought.*

You need to understand we will never know where we are headed in life if we continue to be frantically driven by man-made communication.

In most cases, when we arrive at our *mind-driven* destination and we awaken to the reality of our life's journey, we will realize that our life's mission has reached a *Dead End!*

Therefore, don't simply wake up and smell the coffee. We have over slept. Hence, it is time that we wake up and mindfully sense our lives.

Is this world really an illusion?

<u>*Since some spiritual teachers may answer yes to this inquiry, allow me to clarify what these spiritual teachers may be insinuating*</u>:

It is not the physical landscape and the beauty of this world that we consciously see and encounter within the *present moment* that is an illusion. The illusion only resides within our subconscious mind, which is a man-made world that we often times visit that actually mirrors a world of *make believe.*

Therefore, our man-made world is saturated with *man-made beliefs that our subconscious mind makes us believe*. This in turn manifest into a confusing and complex world that is based upon an *elusive reality.*

Please realize that our uncontrolled or *subconscious* awareness primarily lives within the grief that is contained within our subconscious mind which is an abstract world that really does not exist. Considering the *presence of authentic life* does not reside there— whether we recognize this or not—wherever our thoughts live most will begin to lay the foundation for our reality.

Our thoughts, whether true or not, form our perception which in turn creates what we perceive to be real. In other words, our precious lives are formed based upon what we *subconsciously* think is real.

<u>Please confirm if the following statement is accurate to you. "It is only what we think of our 'selves' that really drives us crazy."</u>

Well, in light of what was just stated allow me to ask you a very sensitive question.

Do you ever wonder why events such as the Connecticut School Shooting, Colorado Theater Massacre, Columbine Shooting, among other numerous acts of appalling violent crimes take place? Are you dying to know what drives a person to this cliff of mental insanity?

It seems no matter how much we think or try to seek a logical answer for these heinous acts of violence we are still left without an answer. The real reason I feel we are left scratching our heads is because we are all trying to conjure up a rational explanation from a madness that is totally irrational.

Chapter III

See, being more aware of what truly defines us, creates a more loving and *rational subconscious mind*; whereas, being *unaware* of who we are, tends to construct a more destructive and *irrational subconscious behavior.*

Our human havoc is a direct byproduct of us not knowing who we are. And through this absence of knowing we fail to control our man-made self which is responsible for this mental mayhem. This is why certain individuals within humanity will continue to be stimulated by this heinous behavior; unless they discover how to tame this *man-made beast* that we call; *"The Human Ego!"*

Now speaking of the human ego, do you realize our ego manages our thoughts? Did you know what we think about our 'selves' means everything? In other words, do you know that what we think about our 'selves' determines how we feel about our 'selves'?

Did you know, based upon how we perceive our 'selves', this unclear perception can weigh us down and drive us crazy?

This leads me into the next question.

<u>Did you know that humanity suffers from two types of egos: a superior ego and an inferior ego</u>?

See, the way our egos work, anyone whose thoughts are possessed and controlled by their subconscious mind will become victimized by their ego.

As we all know, the superior egoist sufferer displays a pseudo self-image, which has been deemed very *noticeable* by society. These individuals are outgoing and obnoxious and are labeled as your *quintessential egomaniacs.*

Now there's also your inferior egoist sufferer, whom no one seems to care about or even *knows about.* However, what makes these *invisible souls* more detri**mental** to society is that society fails to bear witness to the festering manifestation of an *ego* within these outcast beings.

Once again, please note any human being who is not aware of his true essence will unfortunately suffer from some form of an ego.

Now, what's interesting is that although the quintessential egomaniac can be annoying, they're not a real threat to society. Since, beneath their facade, they are typically concealing the fear of feeling inferior.

In contrast, the inferior egoist sufferer or *ego-insaniac* is a HUGH hazard to society. Their inferior perception of themselves is what tends to drive them insane.

These individuals are characters whose synthetic self-image is not admired by our man-made societies. Thus, this exclusion from society begins to submerge these secluded individuals into a state of mental depression and isolation.

Unfortunately, as time passes and ill thoughts of hate and insignificance begin to permeate throughout the victims' subconscious minds, this method of subconscious thinking convinces the ego-insaniacs that their lives are meaningless.

See, based upon society's disapproval of the ego-insaniac's ill-fitting self-image, the ego-insaniac has in turn appraised him *'self'* as being worthless and therefore useless to society.

Now, this perception of condemnation which the ego-insaniac believes has been passed down to them by society begins to plague these lonely individuals, leaving them with an image of low self-esteem and shallow self-worth.

This dismal perspective of one's rejected self-image tends to make the ego-insaniac despise not only themselves, but unfortunately humanity as a whole.

Therefore, through their mental anguish and suffering they begin to take their man-made conditioning personally and proceed to blame society for their pain. Hence, all of humanity must now pay a price for the ego-insaniac's *misperception* of a society assigned suffering. The moral of this very sad story is that the only reason we reject the way another human being appears is because the loving essence of this Universe is not mindfully clear.

What I find interesting is that when someone seems to go insane we tend to believe that this is the result of an individual who has *lost their mind.* However the irony is, when a human being snaps and goes "crazy" their mind is far from being lost. This is not the outcome of a soul who has lost his mind; this is the byproduct of a precious soul whose attention has been *completely lost and trapped within the darkness of his subconscious mind.*

If we were to quiet our subconscious minds and *lend our heart an ear*, we would hear a silent whisper that would say; *my children, the truth to all you seek, solely rest within here.*

Do you know why certain human beings believe that they are above other human beings?

See, the higher our egos elevate us into believing our material worth determines our true value, the more apt we are to believe that our egoist accomplishments are what make us better than other human beings.

In other words, the higher we hover or stand upon our egoist achievements, the more likely we are to believe that those who are materially deprived are beneath us.

Do you know there is really no such thing as material value?

Of course, we can't ignore the fact that modern man lives in an overwhelmingly material world. Nevertheless, this does not mean we should be a part of the world's carnal consumption. The key goal is to learn how to *appreciate* all things—*yet become associated with nothing.*

However, through our manipulating man-made dialogue, we have inserted our *total self-worth* into all material objects and man-made concepts. Consequently, when the material commodity loses its novelty and starts to depreciate so does our *self*-investment.

See, we need to make a personal withdrawal of any affiliation with material objects and project the value of *gratitude* for what we have whether it's old or new. And it would also be nice to top it off with a little *appreciation* too.

Thus *gratitude and appreciation* are the two most *priceless emotions* that give value to any material item.

Do you know every single day someone is bidding for our thoughts?

In truth, I don't sense humanity as a whole realizes how valuable or *invaluable* our thoughts really are. I don't feel we honestly know that it is only our thoughts that grant value to any material item. This is why, around the clock, we have commercials, infomercials, radio advertisements, magazines, politicians, etc., all trying to *cash in* on our thoughts. Hence, many groups and individuals are only interested in one thing and that is *"What We Think!"*

Question: Why is an exotic sports car so expensive? Why are the latest electronic gadgets so costly? Better yet, why is a 'diamond' a shiny stone from the Earth's surface so darn pricey?

Well, the answer to all these questions is quite simple; *because we think so.*

See, through our beliefs, we are under the impression that the true value of life only lives in a *better monetary tomorrow,* which makes us work desperately towards achieving certain material items.

We have all been deceived into believing that these material accomplishments will ultimately provide us with a better life. Only to harshly realize, that every material object that we relinquish our lives for, in order to achieve a *brief sense of happiness*, is actually fleeting in nature. Hence, every material item, regardless of the size of its price tag, will eventually lose its novelty.

Beyond what we think, we are not in search of the material item itself. However, we are indeed looking for the *feeling* that we believe will be associated with this material merchandise and nothing more. And, I am certain that the only feelings that we seek in life are *love, peace, and joy*. I am 100% certain that there are no human beings intentionally pursuing *fear, worry, hate, anger, and depression*.

Nonetheless, our beliefs have convinced us that the sacred emotions of *love, peace, and joy* can only be achieved through material items and material worth. When in truth, if you really think about it, there is actually *nothing material* about the divine feelings of *love, peace, and joy*.

Do you discern based upon what we think, that we will experience either feelings of love or misery? In other words, do you realize via our thoughts, we are the only ones responsible for how we feel?

See, we human beings are designed with the gift of free will. This means *we are free to 'think' as we will, in order to determine how we feel*. Therefore, we have been given dominion to create loving feelings upon demand. This, my friend, is what makes us human beings, just a tad bit more special than any other living Being on this planet that we call Earth.

Mammals in general have been given the instinctive nature to express love physically. However, as it relates to us human mammals, *we have been blessed with a subconscious mind that heightens our sensation and ability to love.* And to make matters even more glorious, we human beings are the only creatures on this divine planet that are blessed with the conscious capacity to create our own *loving reality via thought.*

Nevertheless, we choose to create our own human suffering, by way of disrespecting the love that lives within us, as well as, disregarding the gift of love that lives within the present moment by telling the *existing moment* to hold on for a moment because I am in search of a *better 'present' tomorrow.*

If we human beings continue to waste our precious lives, by living in the future, via our misguided attention, then we will always be consumed by the two most dreadful emotions that are not in harmony with our true nature which are *fear* and *worry.*

If we only live for an imaginary moment that may never exist *then we will forever fear and worry what tomorrow will bring.*

<u>*Please attempt to grasp the following*</u>:

The presence of real life will forever be present and will always be awaiting our full attention. However, as it stands now; if the present moment is not satisfying our *man-made needs* then the present moment is deemed as pointless and therefore ignored.

Now, it is finally time to address whether or not the human species is the only life form privy to consciousness and thought.

So, are we human beings the only conscious species on this planet or are there other creatures that also display consciousness? If so, are these non-human life forms also capable of thought?

In other words, is an insect or animal such as a bee, bird, cat, or dog, for an example, conscious and qualified to produce thought?

Chapter III

Well, here is my answer:

As I mentioned at the top of this chapter, there is no doubt that every living form of life on this *conscious planet bears awareness*. However, as it relates to thinking I do sense that every other non-human life form thinks *instinctively* versus rationally.

Let's use man's best friend as a prime example:

Dogs may not be aware of certain man-made concepts or material things such as brand name cars, the latest fashions, and what country they reside in. And they surely don't waste their time *thinking* about whether or not I have a *bigger tail* than yours. They cannot see beyond the present moment. In other words dogs are not plagued with *worrying about yesterday and concerning themselves with tomorrow*. They are also not aware that their physical form will inevitably expire; therefore, they do not *fear death* in the same manner as we do.

And speaking of our physical forms expiring, why do we human beings fear the inevitable? Since, fearing the inevitable is not going to make the inevitable less inevitable.

See, we human beings are so 'worried' about our man-made sense of self-dying that we 'fear' to live.

Okay, let's get back to man's best friend. Dogs also do not suffer from *self-awareness*. In other words, dogs are not *self-conscious* of a *physical image* that really doesn't define them. Additionally, dogs have not been *conditioned* to view and hate other dogs strictly based upon a difference in physical form.

But please don't think for a second because a dog is not conscious of the *irrelevant* things in life that we human beings are *subconsciously* consumed with means that dogs have no conscious awareness at all.

Is Your 'Self' The Ruler Of 'Your' Thoughts?

<u>*Thus I ask you, what is the benefit of consciousness and thought if we human beings have no Earthly idea how to effectively use either*</u>?

See, dogs experience their world *consciously in the present moment* through their senses. They see, hear, smell, and taste their world. They remember where they have been. They recognize sounds. They may like some people or things and dislike others. Dogs may at times display anxiety; but for the most part they exude excitement. When dogs sleep they appear to dream, their bodies twitch as if they have sensed something intriguing. They clearly are not just an organic machine that is without any inner or conscious experience.

Now, in regards to instinctive thinking, notice how your dog stares and listens to you. Notice how they can be trained to obey your commands. See, all this *instinctive behavior* requires *instinctive thought.*

<u>*In my opinion, dogs are considered "man's best friend" for an essential reason and here's why*</u>:

Man's Best Friend has a genuine loving nature and man's best friend does not suffer from a *"Dog Gone Ego!"* Could this be the primary reason why some of us love our dogs more than we love Thy neighbor?

The reason we human beings are so connected to dogs is because they display an intuitive way of uplifting our spirits.

The soul of a dog is always present and always conscious. A dog is never distracted with notions of yesterday or tomorrow. A dog is always waiting for us in the *existing moment* with their *undivided attention.* In other words, dogs always exist in the *here and now.*

Therefore, in light of a dog's constant awareness of the current moment, the soul of a dog is able to manifest itself through a dog's behavior in divine like qualities such as *loyalty, caring, playfulness, and excitement.* And to top it all off they mostly display a true sense of *unconditional love.*

Thus, this is the *core* reason why humanity harvests such a strong love and affection for our four legged best friend.

Despite what we may believe, our emotional bond with our dog is not the result of a *physical connection;* because during this soulful interaction our ego is turned off. Hence, this is the product of a *soulful relationship,* which illuminates the real essence of who we are.

Take a second to decipher a dog's name from end to start and it will be clear as to why the soul of a dog touches the core of the human heart. *Dog spelled backwards is God.*

It seems based upon all the turmoil we go through as lost souls a dog appears to be the Universe's interim gift to us as a token of peace and love, as we desperately try to persevere through the man-made madness that currently corrupts our subconscious minds and causes our internal suffering.

As we reflect on the information I have shared thus far, no matter what we have been conditioned to believe, there is no such thing as a dumb animal, considering an animal's behavior is *instinctively* what it is. However, as it relates to us human beings . . . well now, that's an entirely different story.

Do you know that we are the 'conscious observer' that produces thought?

When we are in total control of our awareness we tend to have placid thoughts. And through these warm thoughts there is a certain peace and tranquility that is bestowed upon our human form.

The human body tends to be calm, due to the absence of *man-made turbulence.* This genuine awareness of who we are begins to resonate throughout our human framework as being the truth.

When we possess a true sense of who we are, we will always question what our man-made paradigm has to say.

However, when we are on the cusp of sensing who we are, our awareness is interrupted by man-made instruction. Thus, our true essence tends to fight and struggle with this information.

When we receive a divine feeling from this Universe this honest sensation tends to permeate throughout our entire human structure. When this trustworthy feeling collides with unreasonable man-made doctrine, this in turn creates a *neutral emotion* commonly referred to as *confusion*. The expected result is that our cerebral battle with our man-made paradigm is associated with the bewilderment surrounding our mysterious identity, as well as, what is *our soul's purpose* for being here.

Do you know for the most part we seldom control how we feel?

Therefore, I have a question for you: Why do we choose to grant other people the authority to make us feel a certain way?

What I find interesting is what we think of our 'selves' really isn't based upon what we think at all. Considering, it is usually based upon what others think.

<u>For an example</u>:

No one intentionally chooses to feel bad about them 'selves'. Although, the moment someone projects their negative opinion towards us we have the choice to either accept this unfavorable opinion as our reality or reject it because it does not comply with our personal perception.

Nevertheless, we tend to *co-sign* these *exterior thoughts* that are usually laced with ill intentions, which in turn, means we have *authorized* another human being to make us feel in an incongruent manner.

Chapter III

Does changing our thoughts really change our lives?

I know it is often said, that if we learn how to change our thoughts then we can actually change our lives. However, I am going to challenge this belief and say that our thoughts really do not change the 'natural nature' of our lives.

<u>And why you may ask</u>?

If *life* is what really defines us and if life itself is an *unchangeable* force of nature, *then this must mean our true nature is not created to vary.* As it relates to the true nature of life, life itself is *static*. Therefore, life itself *cannot be altered*. Hence, life itself is sacred; *thus, life is what it is.*

In reality, we are all *sacred forms of conscious life*, which means the true essence of who we are is not subject to change. So, changing our thoughts will not *technically* change the *untouchable* nature of our lives. However, a change in thought will transform our perception of what we *think* the 'concept' of life is. Which means, this will in turn alter the physical experience that we have with the *idea* of life itself.

As stated above, we are all sacred forms of conscious life, which means it is only *formless life* that defines us all. Therefore I ask you, once our sacred life comes to an end, then what is left of who we *think* we are?

See, as it stands now, as we compare our *man-made self* to our *sacred life* our man-made image is tipping the scale. However, when our *formless life has moved on,* all that is remaining of our human form is an *empty shell.*

IV

Are We Only Human Or Are We Only Life?

I know based upon some of the mindless things we human beings tend to do in life, we often use the following excuse, to excuse us from our human behavior: *Well, I am 'only' human!*

Well, are we really only human, or are we technically the 'energy' of life?

What if I were to tell you, that you don't have a life because in reality you are life.

<u>*Life has always been considered an enigma; so I ask you, are 'we' the mystery of life?*</u>

Before you answer this question, allow me to ask you this, "Is the true nature of who we are also a mystery?"

Regardless of how you answered these questions, let me ask you this, "Do you see the correlation here?" Do you detect that there could be an immense possibility that there's indeed a connection between the mystery of life and our conscious nature?

Chapter IV

Once we uncover the divine nature of whom we are, we will concurrently reveal the *eternal* mystery of life. In other words, once you discover the true you, life will no longer be a secret. Once you tap into this level of knowing, you will understand that you are simply the divine energy of *conscious life*.

Did you know every form of nature contains the energy of formless life? In other words, do you sense, that our true nature is indeed life itself? Do you know that we are a more rational form of consciousness? Or in other words—a more advanced form of life? If so, do you realize one of the most essential things that can be attributed to our conscious advancement is <u>love</u>?

Unlike any other form of nature on this planet, we human beings have been gifted with the divine ability to experience love on a more conscious and compassionate level.

With this being said, does a piece of you at least discern that 'love' is our only true emotional nature? Do you acknowledge that without love, life itself is meaningless? If so, then ask your 'self' this very serious question. Ask your 'self', "Why does it make 'us' hate, if love is our true impassioned nature?"

The simple answer is that the attention we robotically relinquish to our *'selves'* has conditioned us to hate through blindly believing that we as human beings should hate certain things, as well as, certain people that are not in compliance with our *man-made perception of self.*

Thus, our man-made paradigms have deceivingly educated us on an artificial life and through this fake diplomacy our subconscious mind has placed us in detention from the truth which *resides above and within us.*

You see, our egos have deceived and distorted the manner in which we live in such a way that life lived in the form of *only* human appears to be evil.

Now, as *wholly* human beings, we are born to *live* and *love*. However, through the twisted teaching of our egos we have *evolved* into *evil.*

Do you recognize when we fail to consciously love, we allow our paradigms to trigger hate? And once our subconscious mind stimulates our human form with this treacherous feeling do you realize how damaging this is to our physical health?

Please understand any *negative feeling* that is generated from our paradigms is actually not in harmony with our true nature. We human beings harbor many negative beliefs that lead to pessimistic emotions. These adverse emotions subconsciously percolate throughout our human form and tend to create a feeling of disharmony within our physical framework and also throughout the entire Universe.

Each negative feeling inflicted upon our human form does tremendous damage to our human DNA. In other words, every unfavorable feeling bestowed upon the human anatomy has pathological consequences.

So, with this being said, do you believe that our human DNA is what officially defines who we are as human beings?

Most human beings view our DNA as the authentic blueprint to who we are. However, our DNA does not represent the *intangible conscious energy that defines our real nature.*

Our DNA is in the form of long macromolecules, which comprise our human chromosomes and which provides the mechanism of transmitting our 'evolving' genome from one generation to the next.

Our DNA are large molecules found in all of our cells which encode the genetic instructions for the development and functioning of our bodies. The *soul of this Universe* is the *immortal*

Chapter IV

real essence of refined purity that rests solely within every cell in our bodies.

Thus, the *soul energy* of who we are is what really defines our *conscious life* and is the *true blueprint* to our loving selves.

Based upon what has been stated above, I am going to presume that you realize there is only one feeling that is congruent with our true nature and that is the divine feeling of love.

So, with this being said, let me ask you a question: When we experience love, is there any better feeling?

See, our primary purpose for living is to *love*. And whatever else we accomplish while we are here is nothing more than a secondary purpose. Love is indeed our natural nature. Hence, love is what we are all in pursuit of because love is what creates the genuine feelings of peace and joy. Thus, *love is our life's purpose*. And if we never *purposefully* love then guess what? We will never know the true meaning of life.

<u>Therefore I ask you, isn't our whole reason for 'Being' designed to love life?</u>

Well then, if you are someone who loves life, then guess what? You would naturally love me, considering I am a form of life. Therefore, in reality, if you say that you love life, in essence you are confessing to love this world, and every living 'Being' within it because the truth of the matter is, this entire world is nothing more than a Global form of life itself.

Do you believe everything we fear is justifiable?

Well, if your answer is no! Then you really need to ask your 'self' the following question: Why does our 'self' make us fear, what may not be warranted?

See, in reality, regardless of what we may believe, *fear is not based upon reality*. Fear is only a man-made concept that we have been conditioned to believe is real. And although we should be cautious of real danger, I am sure it is safe to say that most of our beliefs that we *subconsciously fear* are far from fatal.

Thus, we only fear our beliefs that lurk within our subconscious mind. Considering, our subconscious mind is where we spend the most of our time; this is why we live such a *fearful and destructive life.*

The truth of the matter is we do not fear the genuine nature of life, we only fear the nature of our thoughts that dwell upon man's self-demeaning version of life.

See, our paradigms are established based upon a *'make believe'* world. This means our subconscious mind is comprised of beliefs, ideas, theories, and concepts that man has *'made us believe'* are worthy of the truth. If you desire to escape this make believe world, then you will need to ascertain how to shift your awareness towards authentic life. Only then will you discover the nature of pure reality.

Upon this enlightening discovery, you will know that there is actually nothing to fear. This will bring true meaning to the phrase: *"exiting the darkness and entering into the light."*

Although our awareness is guaranteed to drift back into the man-made darkness, our responsibility is to recognize where our awareness inadvertently wanders and steer it back into a more pleasant place.

For every unfavorable journey that our awareness takes within our subconscious mind we will need to make sure that it is a brief trip.

Do you realize fear is not an emotion that we consciously choose? Do you know if we do not consciously make a choice, our subconscious mind will automatically make a decision for us?

Thus, any automatic or *subconscious* emotion, that is provoked and is not in compliance with the essence of love, is actually a warning signal that is used to alert us that we need to make an immediate adjustment in our perception.

See, *fear is a subconscious emotion* that has been created by our respective societies. Fear is a disabling emotion which has been implanted within our subconscious mind to impede the progress of our lives. Fear is the most controlling man-made emotion ever formed within the subconscious minds of humanity.

Fear is disharmonious; fear is destructive; fear is debilitating. Fear is what makes us fear our *'selves'*. And, fear is the primary emotion which we live by. Yet the irony is even though we know how catastrophic this dreadful emotion is, *we still fear change.*

As I previously stated, fear is a man-made illusion. Fear originates and dwells within the top floor of our subconscious mind. And it is only due to our uncontrolled consciousness that dwells upon this crippling emotion that makes our man-made fears feel so real.

As I mentioned earlier, love is the only authentic emotion that is stored within the heart of every human being. Love is uplifting and constructive. Hence, love is what constructs a true sense of peace and harmony within our lives. Love is the only emotion that is in alignment with our true nature.

In other words; love is *official*, love is *real*. Love *is the only emotion that we 'naturally' feel.*

In light of this divine emotion that we call love, let's talk about love and religion. Now, although I am not one who is fond of the man-made concept of this Universe that is constructed by religion, I must be fair and give credit, where credit is due.

Therefore, as it relates to religion and love, if you happen to be a *healthy* religious believer, you may have matured into a very caring, considerate, and loving human being through the love that you have formed, by way of worshipping your Religious version of this Universe.

Thus, through the admiration that you have developed for your religious God, the divine energy of love may have grown enormously strong within your human body.

Now, once the nature of love begins to blossom within your human form, a *feeling of truth* also begins to rise with it. However, there is a sad ending to this very beautiful story. Unfortunately, we human beings do not realize that this *energy of love* or this *feeling of truth* is actually the *rise of us!*

And although the concept of religion has the potential to transform us into more loving human beings, unfortunately, our religious belief will never possess the power to *free the spirit of who we are*. Simply because the more powerful this feeling of love expresses itself within our human form, the more our religious belief convinces us that this distinguishable feeling of truth only represents the presence of our *Religious* version of this Universe, versus the *true nature of who we are*.

<u>And do you know why we believe that this glorious feeling of truth only exemplifies our Religious version of God and not us</u>?

Well, it's because we only perceive our 'selves' as being <u>only human</u> and as nothing more. And if we continue to believe that our <u>material</u> form is all that *matters,* then this man-made notion will forever make us *fear* the idea of being one with this *intangible* energy of certainty that we believe only exemplifies *man's* religious version of this Universe.

Thus, if we proceed to characterize our *'selves'* as being only human, then it will become virtually impossible for us to ever perceive our 'selves' as *'Being'* more divine. Meaning, the true spirit of who we are will never *rise and shine* and be completely free from our man-made *'selves'* until we break free of our *restrictive* religious convictions.

<u>*Here's the fundamental difference between fear and love*</u>:

Fear destroys all that is good but love conquers all that is bad. Therefore, if we really want to conquer our fearful beliefs then we will need to come to the sound *conscious conclusion* that love is the only divine emotion that defines us.

Once we all recognize this degree of knowing as being our true impassioned nature, this world will become *fearless*. This will naturally create a world filled with love and harmony.

In order to achieve peace within us, we will need to become more cognizant of the feelings that are being administered within our body. The essential clue is to recognize all thoughts that are manifesting into feelings of disharmony within us. Any disharmonious feeling is a direct contradiction to our true loving nature.

Therefore, the rise of any incongruent feeling within our human form is a clear indication that we are not in conscious control of our thoughts. Our anatomy will tell us so, based upon certain feelings of distress.

See, there is only one way to distinguish whether or not our beliefs are lying to us. And that distinction is based upon a consequence of how *terrible they make us feel*.

So, whenever our form is being attacked by negative or uncomfortable feelings, we need to promptly intervene and redirect our thoughts into a more loving space in order to restore a more harmonious feeling within us.

Do you know that beyond our limiting subconscious beliefs we are all boundless conscious Beings?

Conscious life is the genuine nature that defines every living organism. Thus, conscious life is what brings true meaning to every physical form. In other words, *beneath the surface* of it all, we are all the essential energy of *conscious life.* This means the life that resides within your human form is no different than the universal life that exists within any other living species on this planet.

Therefore, no matter what we human beings may believe, the life that resides within us is no more valuable than any other form of life. Considering, this would have to be construed as an oxymoron as if to say, *"Life is more sacred than itself."*

In order to know the true meaning of life, we must first acknowledge that it is only *conscious life* that defines us. When we comprehend this sacred understanding, we will begin to have a true love and respect for all forms of life. Thus, this divine awareness will bring true meaning to, *"treat another living Being as you would treat your **true** self."*

As long as we are held hostage by our subconscious beliefs by believing that I am *White* and you are *Black* or I am *Hispanic* and you are *Asian,* then this method of *divisive thinking* will never allow one human to passionately treat another human as they would treat themselves.

Considering, perceiving another form of life through this narrow perspective, makes it practically impossible for us to see our personal form within the framework of another human being that blatantly contradicts our man-made self-image.

<u>*Here is a brief exercise that can be used in order to connect with the reality of life*</u>:

Allow me to say that gaining control of our consciousness is not an easy task. It is going to require tremendous patience and dedication on our behalf. Therefore, in order to gain conscious control of your life, you must take baby steps. What I am suggesting you do, in order to plug into reality is, periodically, throughout any given day, grant the present moment at least 15 to 30 seconds

Chapter IV

of your undivided attention. Eventually, you will notice how your conscious awareness will amplify. And once your attention reaches a certain level of coherency, this state of cognizance would then mean that you have finally become aware of your own awareness.

This is when you will sense the soul of who you are peeking through the windows of your human form. Thus, *the eyes of the human form are the windows to the soul of who we are.*

Please note, this conscious exercise of 15 to 30 seconds can be performed at any time during the day. Meaning you can be running, walking, driving, brushing your teeth, taking a shower, etc.

At any given point during your day, you owe it to who you are, to take intervals of at least15 to 30 seconds to consciously reconnect with official life. And trust me, when you start granting your full awareness to the peaceful present and stop lending it to the rambunctious past and future, you will begin to develop a better feel for genuine life, as well as, establish a keener sense for the conscious essence of who you really are.

These 15 to 30 seconds of entering into the present moment is simply an abbreviated form of meditation.

Now, as you are relishing in the present moment with complete awareness, make sure your physical senses are also turned on and locked into the moment. In other words, be completely conscious of what you see, hear, smell, touch, and taste.

If you happen to be enjoying a meal, as you are performing this conscious exercise, then please make sure that you are *coherently enjoying* your meal. Meaning, please make a conscious attempt to be one with your meal through tasting and experiencing the texture of your food. Also consciously embrace the aroma of what you are eating. And then notice how different your meal appears , taste, and smell once it has your *total engrossed attention.*

In other words, it is important to make sure that you are *deliberately aware* of everything that is transpiring within the moment, as well as, what is taking place within your human form. Become fully engaged with how you are *physically interacting* with each and every moment you lend your awareness to in order to get a real feel for reality.

However, here's the caveat, during the early stages of performing this conscious exercise, it is important when you decide to take time to visit and be in sync with the present moment; it is best that you are not in the presence of another human.

Why you may ask?

Well, because it is usually difficult to appreciate the present moment in the presence of another person's ego. This is because our disharmonious egos interfere with the harmony that resides within the reality of the present moment. Therefore, if one's ego is not subtracted from the present moment then this will usually equate to a non-peaceful encounter with authentic life. Please note this statement also applies to your ego as well.

Therefore, in the absence of one's ego; we notice how beautiful and peaceful life truly is.

The irony is, the *"After Life"* that we human beings seek, will only *present* itself, *'after'* we stop believing in man's *troublesome* version of life.

Chapter IV

**The True Mystery of Life**

The mystery of life is so profound and no matter what we may think it cannot be defined as a noun.

It is this precious mystery of life that makes our loving heart sing. However, in its natural essence it cannot be described as a person, place, or thing.

Life is not a temporary material presence; it is an everlasting incorporeal essence.

As it relates to our vast conscious Universe, life is the most vital component. Yet, there is only one space where life can really be embraced and that is within the present moment.

Without life, life itself would have no true meaning. Considering, it's only life that provides us with that oh so loving feeling.

We are conditioned to think that life is defined by what we materially possess; which is why our lives resemble such a stressful mess.

We believe that our human form represents the true nature of our life. Thus, when our man-made perception of 'self' is dead and gone, our true sacred identity will still live on.

Only through manifesting a true oneness with life, will this create a real sense of peace and harmony throughout our Universe.

However, until then, humanity will forever remain cursed.

So, no matter what your man-made paradigm makes you think or do, there will always be one essential element that stands true. The Sacred Mystery of Life will forever be the soul energy of 'you'!

Despite our man-made conditioning, there's definitely more to us than meets the eye. However, until we encounter that we were born profound we will always seek *external validation through a noun.*

In other words, we will always rely on a *person, place, or thing* to bring some sort of meaning to our lives.

Therefore, please know it is only our distracted *awareness that lounge upon man-made ideas* that conceal the true beauty of life. However, it is indeed the *'miracle of life'* that makes us all *'miraculous' human beings.*

V

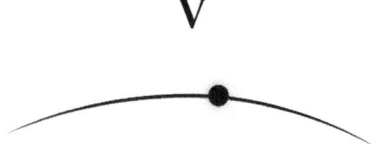

Is Consciousness More Than Just a Mind?

Do we really have a conscious mind?

Well, I feel this is a vital question that begs to be *deeply* explored. However, before you and I suit up and take a deep dive into this vast sea of the human unknown let's first swim towards what many have defined as our conscious mind.

Consciousness is considered the state of being aware of an external object or something within oneself. It has been defined as sentience; the ability to feel, perceive, or to experience subjectively. Consciousness has been deemed as wakefulness, having a sense of selfhood, and the executive control system of the human mind.

Despite the difficulty in definition, many philosophers believe that there is a broadly shared underlying intuition about what consciousness is.

Max Velmans and Susan Schneider wrote in *The Blackwell Companion to Consciousness*: "Anything that we are aware of at a given moment forms part of our consciousness, making conscious experience at once the most familiar and most mysterious aspect of our lives."

Chapter V

Philosophers since the time of Descartes and Locke have struggled to comprehend the nature of consciousness which has made it difficult to pin down its essential properties. Some issues of concern in the philosophy of consciousness include whether the concept is fundamentally valid; whether consciousness can ever be explained mechanistically; whether non-human consciousness exists and if so, how can it be recognized.

Other questionable issues inquire how does consciousness relate to language; can consciousness ever be understood in a way that does not require a *dualistic* approach; which means the mental phenomena are in some respects, non-physical. In other words, can the conscious mind and body *not* be identical? There is also an interesting question as to whether or not it may ever be possible for computers to possess the essence of consciousness.

At one time consciousness was viewed with skepticism by many scientists, but in recent years it has become a significant topic of research in psychology and *neuroscience*. The primary focus is on understanding what it means biologically and psychologically for information to be present in consciousness.

In other words, extensive research is performed on trying to determine how the neural, sub-neural, and psychological aspects of our being correlate with consciousness. The majority of experimental studies assess consciousness by asking human subjects for a verbal report of their experiences (e.g., "Tell me if you notice anything when I do this").

Issues of interest include phenomena such as subliminal perception, blind sight, denial of impairment and altered states of consciousness produced by psychoactive drugs or spiritual or meditative techniques.

In medicine, consciousness is assessed by observing a patient's arousal and responsiveness, and can be seen as a continuum of states ranging from full alertness and comprehension, through disorientation, delirium, loss of meaningful communication, and finally loss of movement and awareness in response to painful stimuli.

Issues of practical concern include how the presence of consciousness can be assessed in severely ill, comatose, or anesthetized people. And how to treat conditions in which consciousness is impaired or disrupted.

Okay, now let's address Sigmund Freud's theory surrounding the human mind. Sigmund Freud believed that our behavior and personality derive from the constant and unique interaction of conflicting psychological forces that operate at three different levels of awareness: *the conscious, the preconscious, and the unconscious.*

What do these terms mean? What exactly happens at each level of awareness?

The human mind according to Freud explains why many of us have experienced what is commonly referred to as a "Freudian slip." These misstatements are believed to reveal underlying, unconscious thoughts or feelings.

Consider this example:

James has just started a new relationship with a woman he met at school. While talking to her one afternoon, he accidentally calls her by his ex-girlfriend's name.

If you were in this situation, how would you explain this mistake?

Many of us might blame the slip on distraction or describe it as a simple accident. However, a psychoanalytic theorist might tell you that this is much more than a random accident. The psychoanalytic view holds that there are inner forces outside of your conscious awareness that are directing your behavior.

For example, a psychoanalyst might say that James misspoke due to unresolved feelings for his ex-girlfriend or perhaps because of misgivings about his new relationship.

The founder of psychoanalytic theory was Sigmund Freud. While his theories were considered shocking at the time and continue to create debate and controversy, his work had a profound influence on a number of disciplines including psychology, sociology, anthropology, literature, and art.

The term psychoanalysis is used to refer to many aspects of Freud's work and research, including Freudian therapy and the research methodology he used to develop his theories.

Freud relied heavily upon his observations and case studies of his patients when he formed his theory of personality development. However, before we can understand Freud's theory of personality, we must first understand his view of how the human mind is organized. According to Freud, the human mind can be divided into three different levels:

The *conscious mind* is what includes everything that we are aware of. This is the aspect of our mental processing that we can think and talk about rationally. A part of this includes our memory, which is not always part of consciousness but can be retrieved easily at any time and brought into our awareness. Freud actually called this the preconscious mind.

The *preconscious mind* is the part of the human mind that represents ordinary memory. While we are not consciously aware of this information at any given time, we can retrieve it and pull it into consciousness when needed.

The *unconscious mind* is a reservoir of feelings, thoughts, urges, and memories that are outside of our conscious awareness. Most of the contents of the unconscious mind are unacceptable or unpleasant, such as feelings of pain, anxiety, or conflict.

According to Freud, the unconscious mind continues to influence our behavior and experience, even though we are unaware of these underlying influences.

Freud likened these three different levels of the human mind to an iceberg. The top of the iceberg that you can see above the water represents the conscious mind. The part of the iceberg that is submerged below the water, yet is still visible is the preconscious mind. The bulk of the iceberg lies unseen beneath the waterline and represents the unconscious mind.

With all this being referenced, the question still remains; does our consciousness really stem from the human brain? And if so, how is it possible that something made of matter is actually capable of producing an energy that contains no matter?

As a matter of fact, I feel we should all ask the following question: Why do we believe that our brain really matters as it relates to exuding our elusive consciousness?

<u>We should all closely examine the following crucial questions</u>:

Do we really have a conscious mind? Or is consciousness more than just a mind? Beyond what we physically see are we indeed the 'unseen' or conscious observer within our human form?

See, what I find intriguing and also ironic is, as it pertains to our religious beliefs, we wholeheartedly believe in the unseen as it relates to the divine energy of this Universe. And we concurrently believe that we are all children of this Universe. So, if we believe that we are the direct offspring of a divine *unseen* universal energy that we refer to as God then why do we struggle with believing that the *unseen* may also apply to us?

<u>Allow me to ask you two meaningful questions</u>:

1. Are we able to *bear witness* to our consciousness?

Chapter V

2. Are we capable of *seeing* our thoughts?

Of course the only answer to both these critical questions is no!

So with this in mind, based upon our acknowledgment of physical or material objects, I am sure it is safe to say that we are the *conscious observer*, as well as, the *producer of thought*, which is both a mysterious and an undiscovered phenomenon.

Therefore, if we are deemed as the conscious observer, as well as, the producer of *untouchable* thought then shouldn't we at least entertain the possibility that we are the *unseen* force behind both these mystifying phenomena?

In other words, it seems to be practical that only an *unseen 'conscious' energy* would have the capability of generating the *untouchable energy(s)* of consciousness and thought.

I am sure you are aware that scientists have yet to uncover the official home of our consciousness, as well as, being able to pinpoint who we really are. Therefore, do you think there could be a reasonable probability that who we are and our consciousness are indeed one in the same? Do you think it could be highly likely, that it's 'only' our consciousness that indeed defines us?

Allow me to ask you another scientific question: If scientists have yet to discover who we are and uncover our consciousness, why do you think we fail to see the irony in this similar oversight. Considering, it seems as if these two intangible forces are inextricably linked?

The biggest puzzle in neuroscience is how the brain activity that we are *conscious of seeing* differs from the brain activity that is driving all of those subconscious actions. It appears obvious that consciousness is what defines us as human beings via our awareness and through our perception of physical life.

When we see a physical object, light stimulated patterns of signals from our retinas travel along nerves as waves of ion driven membrane depolarizations. When they reach the nerve terminus the signal jumps to the next nerve via chemical neurotransmitters. The receiving neurons compute whether or not they will fire, based upon the incoming signal strength and their current state and configurations

In this way signals from our environment are processed in our brain and eventually result in new information, knowledge, and possible physical responses. But where in all this movement of ions, neurotransmitters, and electrical signals is consciousness? *Scientists have not yet identified the processes within the human brain that result in conscious thinking—or even a definitive definition of consciousness.*

Therefore, based upon the high improbability of *physically* locating our consciousness, as well as, who we really are; it appears as if scientists have surrendered their research to a presumption that our consciousness simply stems from the human brain.

Well, do you know why scientists tussle with trying to discover what genuinely defines us, along with exposing our consciousness?

Well, quite frankly the answer to these eerie questions is quite simple. The reason why scientists struggle with defining who we are is because all of their research is focused on defining who we are from a *physical perspective* versus from an *intangible aspect.*

Whether scientist realize this or not, *"seek and you shall find"* has absolutely nothing to do with *eyesight*; however it has everything to do with *insight.*

Since scientists, as well as, the rest of humanity believe that the human brain is the tool that defines us this misconception of knowledge will forever keep our true identity a secret. Considering, we will always be faced with an invalid man-made sense of self.

Chapter V

And as I just mentioned a moment ago, scientists for a lack of conscious discovery, only assume that our consciousness stems from the human brain, simply because our human brain seems to be the most *logical location.*

Inquiring minds may want to know: Can we really be conscious without a brain?

Well, the real question should be: Are we really conscious with a brain?

The brain is a miraculous machine that allows *'you'* the conscious observer, to be *physically in-tune with* the present moment via our five *physical senses of sight, sound, taste, touch, and smell.*

However, it seems based upon all the attention that we grant to our brain through believing that it is the *'gate keeper'* for our consciousness, this presumption robs us human beings of our true conscious potential.

In my opinion, <u>consciousness is far more than just awareness, it's a clear indicator that we human beings are 'alive'</u>.

Hence, we can't be <u>lifeless</u> yet conscious. Our brain development seems to rely on an adequate supply of stimulating consciousness.

We human beings tend to believe that being conscious is simply the state of being 'self' aware which we think grants us the special privilege of being the only conscious species that exist on this planet. To the contrary, it is our *'sub-conscious'* awareness that is fixated on man-made concepts and ideas, that makes us *unconscious* or *unaware* of what is really <u>real</u>. Meaning, we have yet to encounter who we **really** are, and we have yet to experience the **real** meaning of life.

We also seem to think because we are able to *visually* perceive the physical world and form concepts from what we <u>see</u>, this ability to view the world stems from our brain, thus creating our consciousness.

So, the next question should be: Is a 'blind man' really conscious? Well in truth a blind man is more conscious and aware of real life and his real nature than a man who sees.

Although, the human brain is the most amazing tool bestowed upon humanity, I am not sold on the idea that it is responsible for producing our consciousness. From a true conscious perspective it appears that our brain is what I would refer to as a *"concept keeper."* Meaning the brain is a warehouse which 'keeps' and stores our conscious input and then serves as an outlet for all the concepts, ideas, beliefs, and memories that we as conscious Beings think upon and live by.

However, to further define the nature of consciousness, because we human beings have a narrow perspective of what defines the nature of consciousness; this limited awareness is what also minimizes our perception of what truly defines the nature of life or reality.

We human beings are unknowingly loyal to certain words and their presumed meaning, such as the word *unconscious*. Hence, the moment we hear the word *unconscious*; this automatically triggers the belief that a person is <u>completely without consciousness</u>. But, this is not necessarily the case. When a person is deemed as being unconscious; this simply means that they are temporarily *unaware* of the present moment.

In other words, like clockwork, during certain times of the day our brain shuts down our physical senses which makes us unable to sense or be aware of the present moment. However, <u>as long as we are alive and breathing</u> the sacred energy of consciousness is always *present*. Thus, even as we sleep, our body's built-in automatic breathing mechanism ensures that our brain receives the essential energy that 'It' needs in order to function, which I have deemed as the energy of consciousness. But of course, according to man's definition; this energy is only defined as oxygen.

Chapter V

See, we have been conditioned to believe that consciousness is only based upon one's awareness; therefore since we are unaware that the real nature of consciousness is really defined by energy, we lack the necessary <u>*conscious energy*</u> of knowing what actually defines us.

We human beings must realize that Man himself grants *meaning* to everything; which is why we live such a *demeaning* life. Whereas, *consciousness* is the universal *'electromagnetic'* energy that defines and brings *true meaning* to life.

Therefore, as it relates to the current call that has been made on the nature of consciousness, I throw in the red challenge flag and I demand a further review. And I am sure after an extensive review the call that has currently been made on the nature of consciousness will be overturned.

Hence, *who we are*, as well as, our *universal consciousness,* goes far beyond any current scientific *man-made belief.* To elaborate even further, who we are, as well as our consciousness, will always supersede any scientific exploration.

In the field of science, if it is *not detectable or mathematically demonstrable,* then it is *not real.* However, the real irony here is *the intangible energy of consciousness and thought are the only two phenomena that are responsible for creating our tangible reality.* In reality there is *nothing that is more real* within this divine Universe, than the *energy of consciousness.*

The way I envision it, there's no way that our *intangible consciousness* can be *dependent* upon the *tangible brain.* Considering, our consciousness bears its own independence. Thus, the human brain is only the producer of perception; whereas El Sol is the *'independent giver'* of consciousness or in other words—*electromagnetic energy.*

Nonetheless, please do not misinterpret my opinion in regards to science. Through science there have been tremendous accomplishments towards the material advancement of humanity.

Therefore, I take my hat off in all due respect to scientists who have probed and revealed the physical mechanics of the human anatomy among numerous other physical and material achievements.

However, regardless of the nature of one's intellect, if you fail to know who you really are, you will always fall victim to a *limiting belief*.

Because scientists, despite their grand intelligence, thoroughly believe in the concept of *"seeing is believing"* this belief in itself tends to limit the growth of science, as it relates to discovering the residence of consciousness, as well as, who we really are.

In other words, if scientists proceed to believe that they will eventually expose who we are from a *physical viewpoint* then the end result will always be an *absent mind*. Because through trying to tangibly uncover our consciousness, as well as whom we are, *life as we don't know it will still remain a mystery.*

Please know in spite of what we have been conditioned to believe, seeing is *not* believing because in most cases *seeing is deceiving,* considering for the most part, what we *see* is based upon an *ambiguous* man-made reality.

Therefore, if scientists persistently believe that their intellect will one day prevail and they will ultimately *eyewitness* who we are then they will consistently fail to obtain the required wisdom necessary to *envision the intangible truth.*

<u>See, here is the stark difference between intelligence and wisdom</u>:

Intelligence is taught, whereas wisdom is discovered. In other words, our egos represent our intelligence and this Universe personifies our wisdom.

Nevertheless, please do not misunderstand my perspective on intelligence. I am not proclaiming that our intelligence is irrelevant. What I am really trying to convey is wisdom allows us to see or *envision* beyond our intelligence. Or in other words, *wisdom allows us not to be limited by what we have been taught to believe.* Which means, regardless of how smart we think we are our egos are only as intelligent as they have been taught to be.

Therefore, if our ego is never introduced to the true essence of who we are, then in reality our ego has been taught nothing.

So the moral to this passage is, once we marry intelligence with wisdom, we *inspire* an *enlightening* relationship. And with this being said, I once heard a spiritual teacher say, *"In-spire represents 'Being' in-spirit."*

What is the relationship between consciousness and life?

Well, from my perspective, life is a direct byproduct of consciousness. Hence, the energy of *consciousness and life are dependent upon one another*.

For an example, the *untouchable* energy of life cannot exist without the *unseen* energy of consciousness.

Do you discern the '<u>less</u>' control we have of our consciousness, the '<u>more</u>' out of control our life will be?

To some people *uncontrolled consciousness* may sound like an oxymoron. As if to say, "Well if I am conscious, then how can I not be in control of my consciousness?

<u>Well allow me to explain</u>:

Considering humanity is not cognizant of the information that is being processed by our subconscious minds, this unrecognized dependence we have developed for our beliefs has stripped us of our authority to control our own thoughts. This means our paradigms have been able to disable us from controlling our very own consciousness by way of *engaging* us in man-made information. This, in turn, *disengages* us from knowing the truth.

Please permit me to elaborate:

Here's an example of how our man-made paradigms exploit our thoughts:

Since our subconscious mind has no *direct* relationship with the present moment, it is not equipped to provide us with knowledge that is based upon reality. Therefore, the man-made propaganda that our subconscious mind produces, can only share with us; *who we think we are* and *who we think we should be.*

Now, with our thoughts tossed into a past and future vortex. This *non-realistic man-made rhetoric* stored within our subconscious mind distracts us from the existing moment where only *controlled conscious thoughts* should reside.

It is very important that we work towards being more conscious of the present moment so that we can embrace our true nature through the here and now.

In order to be captivated and one with the present moment, we must hold on to it with our *undivided attention.* This means in order for us to experience the *reality of life* in the present moment our awareness must be disconnected from any past or future man-made disturbance. Hence, we human beings must learn how to take a moment—to relish in the moment.

Why is being connected with the present moment so important?

When our awareness is attached to the present moment there is a true sense of *oneness* with all aspects of life and a true feeling of oneness with the energy of who we really are. But most importantly, we have a true sense that we and this Universe are one.

When we are in this conscious state of *Being,* something special begins to unfold. As we reflect upon the present moment, we usually encounter loving feelings and a real sense of *Being* in spirit.

And once our awareness moves back home into the present moment, where it was created to belong, we are more apt to be inspired by new and enlightening ideas. Thus, whether we realize this or not, every moment is refreshing and new.

Now, as I say this please do not misinterpret what I mean; because I am not proclaiming that our awareness should be completely disconnected from our sub-conscious mind. Considering, our sub-conscious mind is connected to this divine Universe, which in turn provides us with constructive information that is indeed useful to us humans for our present and future survival.

However, my core objective is to bring to one's attention, that it is mainly the destructive information that crouches down within the *reactive* area of our sub-conscious mind that often *blindsides* us with detrimental thoughts and emotions that diminish our existence.

Furthermore, I am not trying to convince anyone that life in the present moment was designed to always be a bed of roses, considering as souls of this Universe our human experience while here on earth is to encounter numerous emotions, even if these emotions are not agreeable with our nature. Therefore, we are guaranteed to experience *moments* of pain, sorrow, and frustration. However the goal is to ensure that these moments of despair pertain only to that *specific* moment.

Meaning, if one's past life experience pertains to a destructive and disruptive encounter; then this disturbing moment that has passed, should never be relived or rewrapped. Thus, one should not harbor and unwrap their depressing past in the present moment. When we are dwelling on our past miseries in the present moment, it becomes impossible to embrace an *uplifting* new moment if our past problems are *dragging* us down. In summary, every precious moment of life, should be appreciated and respected for what it is in its purest existence.

Therefore, I ask you to choose to lock the door and throw away the key that grants access into the reactive level of *your subconscious mind.* If we proceed to automatically be stimulated by the *dark-reality* that is currently occupying this level of our subconscious mind, then how can we ever expect to be exposed to *true enlightenment?*

Uncontrolled consciousness tends to create a situation where we are constantly being bombarded with irrelevant and faulty information which is continuously being repeated by our paradigms. Our uncontrolled consciousness makes us think upon what we have been conditioned to believe, *which is the process of dwelling on the past.* It then proceeds to take it a step further by way of steering our attention beyond existing life into a worry filled future.

Hence, this diversion of the present moment is what makes us question whether or not if what we have been conditioned to believe about our '*selves*' will actually be worthwhile tomorrow.

We human beings must recognize that spending our life in the past and in the future is *costly* and that *'Being' conscious* of the present moment is far more *valuable.*

<u>*Do you know what is required to be effective at being conscious?*</u>

Presence!

<u>*And what does presence actually mean?*</u>

Our essence must be conscious of the present moment.

As *conscious Beings,* the *present moment* is the only moment that is supposed to have *our deliberate attention.*

<u>*Why you may ask?*</u>

Chapter V

Well, because the present moment is the only designated home for *reality!*

So, if our attention is consumed by the past or the future, whether we are aware of this or not, we are not experiencing reality.

If we spend a quarter of our life lending our awareness to a moment that has already existed *(a.k.a. the past),* and then we spend the other three quarters of our awareness worrying about an *imaginary moment* that has yet to exist or better yet, an imaginary moment that may never exist *(a.k.a. the future),* then there is no way that we are really experiencing the reality of authentic life.

The energy of life can only be experienced within the present moment. And the only way we can ever be connected to the present moment is through ensuring that our *essence is always present*—hence the true meaning of *presence.*

<u>*Allow me to ask you a thought provoking question: Can we physically smell, taste, touch, see, or hear the past or the future*</u>*?*

Our subconscious mind may allow us to envision certain images as they relate to the past and the future. However, I am sure it is safe to say that there is no *physical* way we can use our senses to have an *'explicit'* experience with a moment that is technically *not real.* Hence, all five of our senses are designed to experience the reality of life only as it exists within the present moment.

Nonetheless, every day we tend to waste our attention trying to encounter moments that are *not alive and authentic.* Therefore, since our five senses are not created to plug into an *artificial* moment we in turn *officially* feel bad. In other words, if our awareness is not fixated upon official life our emotional outcome will always be an incongruent or synthetic feeling.

Now, the initial step towards experiencing the present moment is to first ascertain that *you are indeed the conscious observer* that resides within your human form. This level of awareness will help you to detect a true oneness with life and through this coherency, you will transcend into a natural oneness with the present moment.

After you have observed and embraced the immediate moment, your heart will harmoniously relay a feeling to your subconscious mind which will in turn shower your human form with an emotion that would define how this sacred moment made you genuinely feel.

<u>Please take a moment to consider the following statement because it is very important</u>:

Although our human form is fixated in the present moment, only our awareness determines what moment we are actually experiencing.

<u>Allow me to elaborate</u>:

No matter where we are *physically,* nine times out of ten our attention is not in-sync or present alongside our physical bodies. Often our awareness has taken a distant trip of its own elsewhere.

The destination of our awareness usually makes only one stop, and that is in a corrupt neighborhood within our subconscious mind, which is an environment that is filled with man's twisted version of a *make believe reality.*

This means as I stated earlier, our subconscious mind can only provide us with a moment that has already existed or an imaginary moment that may never exist. Therefore, our subconscious mind will *never* be able to attach us to a bona fide moment that depicts a true sense of *reality*; since as *divine conscious Beings,* this is solely our responsibility.

<u>Here's the problem with visiting the existing moment</u>:

In this day and age our beliefs have flooded over into our present reality. This means we are all living in the present moment in

Chapter V

accordance with the *make believe* concepts that are formulated within our subconscious minds.

Thus, the present moment as we perceive it today, based upon our *subconscious interactions*, seems to be in compliance with our man-made paradigms which unfortunately tend to solidify our man-made beliefs.

However, once we *unmask* who we truly are we will be able to see the grand forest, even beyond the *lying* trees.

If you ever discover that you are indeed merely the *conscious observer*, then even in the midst of everyone else's subconscious existence; the present moment will still be a beautiful place to live.

<u>*In summary, what is the sum value of controlled consciousness?*</u>

In a nutshell, please understand that our frantic lives are a direct result of our *desolate consciousness*. Therefore, since we suffer from a deficient amount of alert awareness, we have yet to figure out how to tap into our own astuteness, in order to engage and partake in life as we *Will*.

Thus, we must comprehend that the true value of life will always equate to the sum total of controlled consciousness.

Please do not think because we are aware of what we have been taught that this <u>subconscious level of awareness</u> qualifies as being a true conscious thought.

<u>So with the above being stated, here is a brief conscious exercise for you</u>:

At this very moment I want you to grant 10 seconds of your awareness to your immediate environment. And the goal here is to observe and appreciate your current surroundings with an *open subconscious mind*. Which means *do not exude one 'blinding' thought*. In other words, cease *all subconscious thinking* and coherently embrace and view the present moment for what it is.

If you are unable to perform this conscious exercise by way of not being able to suppress a subconscious thought, then guess what? You have less control of your life than you thought.

We human beings must realize that life is a *gift* that can only be appreciated in the *present moment.* Thus, we need to cease *blindly* dwelling upon our man-made past and worrying about man's version of the future. Considering the *gift of life* will never reside within our *head,* therefore we need to stop getting so *ahead* of ourselves.

Please grasp; if we are not in command of our consciousness, or our thoughts, then we are not in control of our lives. It is really that plain and simple.

VI

What Does God Mean To You?

For those who believe in God, God *means* everything and quite frankly this would be an accurate belief. Considering, God *is* indeed *everything* and *everything* is God.

Well, wait a minute!

I sense there may be an enormous conflict with my *'vast'* perception of God **'is'** *everything* versus the *'isolated'* religious concept of God **'means'** *everything*.

See, my reference towards God *'is'* everything means the *conscious energy* of this Universe lives within all forms of life. Whereas, the religious concept of God *'means'* everything may *dictate* that God lives only in the form of one thing. Or in other words, this Universe lives only within the *form of* **one image** such as; *Jesus, Allah, Buddha, Jehovah, etc.*

So, does the religious reference to God mean everything translates to mean that our religious version of God means everything to us? If so, then we need to ask our *'selves'* the following crucial question: What do *we* mean to our religious version of this Universe? Considering, the way it stands now, if we do not adore our man-made Gods, then we are considered to be worthless and therefore we will be punished.

Chapter VI

Thus, the religious Gods that we have been conditioned to compliment and praise actually think very little of us and view us human beings as being inept and incompetent.

Oh, and let's not forget about God's *self-published* religious documents that pertain to a variety of different religions which all claim to have the exclusive rights to the sacred truth. Yet, these documents are all written in riddles. And as we attempt to interpret their perplexing dogma the joke appears to be on us, because everyone seems to have a different interpretation of what the truth is, which in turn leaves us human beings befuddled. This may explain why most religions are so difficult to comprehend—not clear and simple for all to understand.

Well, in my opinion, if religion is a real representation of the truth, then when did the truth become so obscure? In other words, if the religious Gods that we have been coerced into worshipping are indeed authentic, then why does humanity still live in such religious confusion and disarray?

Why do the religious Gods who profess to care about us as individuals not *present* themselves and <u>*clearly*</u> communicate with us on a daily basis—or *ever* for that matter? Okay, here's my *two 'sense'* worth as it relates to the alleged religious truth. I sense that the mystery surrounding the Universe's divine message is hidden within the Good Book; *about which I will share more than just my two 'senses', as I elaborate upon this issue in the next two chapters.*

However, as it appears now, *man* has added more than just his two cents as it relates to *the word of this Universe*. And with this being said, I am a true believer in the **universal word**—although please notice that this *word* is not plural.

This means—the only word of this Universe is *LOVE!*

Thus in reality, the true story about this Universe is short and sweet. *The true nature of the Universe is the "Power of Love";*

End of Chapter, End of Verse, and End of the 'man-made' Story! Therefore, *(love) is the one and only word of this Universe that we should all live by.*

So, with all the above being stated, what is your personal definition of this Universe? Do you believe the energy or the life of this Universe only resides in 'one' image that should be 'religiously' worshipped? Or do you believe the Universal energy of Love lives within every human being regardless if we are religious or not? Do you believe that you can build a lasting and loving relationship with the 'vast' nature of this Universe if you only worship a 'secluded idea' of it?

And last, but not least, do you believe 'your' religion represents the only true notion of this Universe?

It seems that those who believe in man's concept of this Universe; perceive this Universe as being a powerful human-like, supernatural being, or as the deification of an esoteric mystical figure. And no human being is considered *one* with this Supreme Being; therefore every human being is subordinate to this benevolent figure.

Within *Christianity* the doctrine of the Trinity states that God is a single Being that exists, simultaneously and eternally as three entities: The Father (the Source, the Eternal Majesty); the Son (who is Jesus of Nazareth, the father in the human flesh); and the Holy Spirit (the spiritual advocate responsible for the immaculate virgin conception). Some people have illustrated this concept by saying that the Father, Son, and Holy Spirit are one yet distinct, in the same way that ice, steam, and water are one, yet distinctly different from each other.

Islam's most fundamental concept is a strict monotheism called tawhid; which means 'oneness.' God is described in the Qur'an as: "Say: He is God, the One and Only; God, the Eternal, Absolute; He begetteth not, nor is He begotten; and there is none like unto Him." Muslims deny the Christian doctrine of the Trinity and

Chapter VI

divinity of Jesus, Son of Nazareth comparing it to polytheism; which is the worship or belief in multiple deities. In Islam, God is beyond all comprehension or equal and does not resemble any of his creations in any way.

Thus, *Muslims* are not iconodules who serve images and are not expected to visualize God. The message of God is carried by angels to messengers starting with Adam and concluding with Mohammad. God is described and referred to in the Quran by certain names or attributes, the most common being Allah or Al-Rahman meaning; *Most Compassionate* and Al-Rahim meaning; *Most Merciful.*

Buddhism, on the other hand, emphasizes the system of causal relationships underlying the universe which constitute the natural order dharma and source of enlightenment. No dependence of phenomena on a supernatural reality is asserted in order to explain the behavior of matter.

According to the doctrine of the Buddha, a human being must study Nature, in order to attain personal wisdom (prajna) regarding the nature of things (dharma). In Buddhism, the sole aim of spiritual practice is the complete alleviation of stress in samsara; which is called nirvana.

Well, if I had to define this Universe I would have to say that I concur with the Buddha. Hence, in my opinion; there is no *man-made image* that reflects the *divine nature* of this Universe. Considering the mystical energy of this Universe lives beyond the surface of what we see.

In other words; my personal definition of this Universe is the loving source of *conscious energy* that represents *all conscious life.*

Despite our religious diversities, we are all divine children of this Universe and I am placing much emphasis on the word **divine**.

Unfortunately, most religious believers are under the assumption that we are not born divine. We are also conditioned to believe that this Universe is a presence that is completely separate from who are. In other words we believe that we are all born *sinners* and should therefore consistently *beg* our Religious God(s) for mercy in order to be saved from the consequences of our sinful nature. And in spite of this man-made impression nothing could be further from the truth.

See, every human being was indeed born as a bundle of *divine joy* and then converted into a *man-made sinner.*

Therefore, if you ask me what is the original sin? I would have to say the original sin is based upon the man-made notion that we are all born sinners; which in turn *denies* our true divinity.

Do you know why our religions condition us to believe that we lack divinity and are not one with this Universe?

It's quite simple; our religions require us to believe in this fraudulent theory because they need our beliefs in order to survive. Religion is a belittling device that weakens us, by making us believe that we are all born sinners. And since we *subconsciously* validate this self-demeaning belief, this level of thinking makes us feel compelled to rely on our religions for *strength.*

We human beings must realize that the only reason we think that we are not born divine is because we have been conditioned to believe that our human forms are what actually define us.

Therefore, since we believe that our human flesh represents who we are, this erroneous conception in turn makes the *divine nature of who we are weak.*

As I have previously mentioned, we are all children of this Universe or in other words offspring of this Universe.

Chapter VI

Heck! You know what?

There's even a better description that more accurately characterizes our relationship with the sacred energy of this Universe. And that is: *We are all the divine* **Heirs** *(airs) of this Universe!*

Now, allow me to explain:

Did you know the 'air' we breathe is conscious life? In other words; do you realize every single breath we inhale is the conscious energy of this Universe? Did you know through every breath we take, the loving energy of this Universe circulates throughout every aspect of our Being and then supplies our human form with the energy of conscious life? Hence, via the *air* we breathe, we are all indeed the *Divine* **Heirs** of this Universe or the *Heirs of Universal Consciousness.*

See, the reference to the *Air of God*, is what I sense spawned the biblical verse of Genesis 2:7. Which states; "Then the Lord God formed a man from the dust of the ground and breathed into his **nostrils** the breath of life, and the man became a *living being*" (NIV). Well, don't we as human beings breathe through our *nostrils?*

In reality every form of conscious life that resides on this planet consumes the 'same' universal air via their nostrils, gills, or by some other breathing method in order to *consciously survive.*

In my opinion, the names and stories represented within the Good Book are nothing more than animated characters used to tell a *story* surrounding *hidden truths* in an animated way; hence the expression *Biblical Stories.*

See, these stories only seem real because we have been thoroughly conditioned to believe that they are. And by way of our religious conditioning we wholeheartedly believe that there is a divine Supreme Being in the *image of man,* squatting in some special space in the sky. And in addition to answering all of our personal prayers; **He** has also found time to Author several *conflicting* religious documents.

See, whether we discern this or not the commonly used pronouns of *He, Him, and His* are very profound. Thus, it is these selected pronouns that solidifies our man-made belief that the essence of this Universe is actually in the form of a man; which has empowered a *selfish man-made version* of this Universe to be *subconsciously* born and nurtured.

If you believe this Universe appears in the form of a 'man' do you concurrently believe that this is why we fight over Him?

Do you know what I find interesting? History indicates that many Wars in the **name** of God have been fought. Well, that is indeed correct. Considering, let's be honest; no one really fights in the name of **'*love!*'**

See, every Religious War ever fought was indeed in the *name* of God. Considering, every Religious War ever fought, was invoked to defend the *man-made name* of this Universe that represented one's elected religion.

Until we discover the divine nature of who we really are, we will never know the real essence of this Universe. In other words, the *blind selfish love* that we have formed for our religious idea of this Universe have left no room to receive and *'feel'* the true loving energy of this Universe.

We must recognize that there is a vast difference between the true 'spiritual' essence of this Universe and our religious interpretation of this Universe. We human beings will never experience the true nature of this Universe as long as we continue to worship our mythical tales of this Universe on the contentious platforms of our religious beliefs.

Chapter VI

In truth, we human beings do not honor and uphold the divine nature of this Universe because we are too busy fighting to protect our man-made idea of it.

Please know there is only one reason why man's religious version of this Universe seems real. And that's because these legendary beliefs are at the center of our attention.

Despite our religious conditioning there is only *'One'* Universe. And every human being, as well as, all other conscious life forms share the same spiritual energy that stems from this one Universe. This means we are all *united* by the same loving energy from one divine source. And although we choose to call this sacred essence God, this divine energy bears no man-made name. This universal energy should not be *religiously* referred to as Jesus, Allah, Buddha, Jehovah, etc.

With all this said, allow me to ask you a very serious question: Do you truly believe we were born or 'destined' to be religious?

Humanity should realize that there isn't a human being born of this planet that was created and destined to be a Christian, Muslim, Jewish, etc. Hence, please know that we were not born to hand over our life to any man-made idea of this Universe. However, many of us have been thoroughly trained to do so. In other words, it is not in our true nature to be religious. And if humanity ever awakens to this level of realization, we will then know that religion needs us more than we need it.

And with this being said, are you aware of the one thing that keeps our religions alive and flourishing?

Religion survives and thrives only off of our *beliefs,* which we were taught and not born with. Thus, since so many of us have given our *entire lives* to our religions, our religions are in turn *full of life.*

Therefore, if you believe in man's concept of a Devil, and you believe that this Devil has the cunning ability to make something *bad* appear in the form of *good (God)*—then behold Religion!

Since our attention has been captured by our religious beliefs, we have in turn failed to sense the real energy of this Universe that lives within all forms of nature.

Well if, according to religion, God is all merciful and all 'loving', then why does religion contradict itself by making us believe that we need to "Fear God's Love?"

In my opinion, we should not fear the loving energy of this Universe; we should only fear our man-made *selves*.

Out of all creations, we human beings are the only species on this planet that is more conscious of *self* than of *soul*—hence the expression: *"Being self-conscious."*

And please understand to the extreme contrary of what we may believe, being more *conscious of self*, in no way means that we human beings maintain the license for being the only conscious species on this planet. Thus, correct me if I am wrong; but it is our *awareness of self* that creates our human suffering.

We human beings are currently under a man-made hell spell. And the only reason we are unaware of this spell is because we are all collectively taking part in it. See, we tend to share different beliefs based upon a difference in physical appearance and culture. Hence, from this diverse perspective, life the way we *individually* perceive it within our sealed paradigms, makes us appear to be drastically dissimilar from one another. Hence, anything that does not comply with our existing paradigm will be viewed as conflicting and will therefore be ignored.

However, if humanity ever awakens to the true loving nature of this Universe, we will then encounter how we are not just one with this Universe, but how we are also *one* with each other, as well as, with all conscious forms of life.

See, every *animated form of life is conscious*, with the exception of us humans, as it relates to what we are conscious of.

Consciousness is defined by *electro-magnetic energy* and not necessarily by what we perceive. However, due to the way we humans mismanage our conscious awareness; we *'only'* have a *subconscious concept* of what we perceive.

All animated forms of life share the same conscious energy that saturates this Universe. And once we humans come to terms with knowing that we *'All'* share the same divine energy with every other form of life, only then will we become harmonious with life and the true nature of consciousness itself.

Once this discernment takes hold, the soul of who we are will no longer fear the loving nature of this Universe and we will then behold how the love of this Universe naturally manifests through us all.

What I find fascinating is when we, as sacred souls, are born into this world, we are taught to love our *selves,* even the Bible tells us to, "Love . . . Thy *Self*" (Matthew 19:19, KJV).

However, the problem *lies* with the fact that we have no real idea who our *true self* is.

And by granting our attention to our '<u>man-made self</u>'; this crippling perception is why we human beings have no *'self'* control.

So, let's expand upon why we human beings lack 'self' control; which in turn makes us the most 'self' destructive creatures on this planet.

We human beings will never be able to control our *'selves'*, as long as we *believe* that our *'selves'* define who we are. In other words; *we* will never possess the knowhow of gaining control of our *'selves'*, as long as *we* continue to believe that *we* and our *selves* are one in the same.

Until we recognize our true identity we will always be connected with our man-made sense of self. This means we will never be able to think for our *'selves'* therefore our *'selves'* will always think for us and be the composer of our reality.

If we as *sacred souls* continue to believe that our *human form* **possesses** *a soul;* then we as the *soul observer* will forever endure tremendous pain and sorrow as we lie trapped within this agonizing man-made world of *make believe* that has been constructed in our minds. It is only our man-made perception of *self* that *makes us believe* that the human flesh defines who we are and through this fraudulent impression of *self* our paradigms are able to devour our divine power.

So, until we gain *sole/soul* control of a tool that was given to us to possess, it will forever possess us. Therefore, as sacred Beings of this Universe we must realize that our subconscious mind is our possession. However, if we fail to grasp this essential understanding, our subconscious minds will be responsible for our *'self'* destruction. As I mentioned earlier, there is no reason to fear this Universe, only our man-made *selves*. The loving essence of this Universe is not going to destroy us; considering we are leaving this self-destructive task up to our *'selves'*.

We are all born with *free will*. This means we have been given the choice to choose *Peace, Love, and Harmony* which can only be achieved through acknowledging our divine nature. But due to our obscured view of our true loving nature, we have chosen *Violence, Hate, and Disharmony* which are the key ingredients of the recipe for *Self-Destruction!*

By granting our egos the leeway to make us *Hate* and *Fear* other human beings who have an antagonistic resemblance to our human reflection we have become the most *self-destructive* creatures on the planet.

Please be aware that our subconscious mind is the most *powerful tool* ever bestowed upon humanity. Thus, for our own good, we need to learn how to use this glorious gift for *good (God)* and not for *evil (Devil)*.

I AM THAT; I AM says God!

I AM the energy of *life;* I AM the energy of *love;* I AM the energy of this *Universe;* I AM the energy of **everything!**

Once we come to the sound conscious conclusion that what really defines us is a *conscious energy* and *not* a physical *image,* only then will we be able to free *who we are* from our man-made *self.* Unfortunately, as it exists now, we human beings suffer from a horrible case of being extremely *'self'* conscious. And being self-conscious is the process of identifying more with one's *man-made self-image* rather than their *universal nature, which is love.*

If we continue to live our lives allowing our self-images to represent us, then this means we will forever surrender our sacred life to the rules of our man-made societies. There is not a human being on this planet that has been accurately labeled. And, considering we have been tagged based upon our man-made image, we must now comply and behave according to the way we have been *inappropriately* branded.

Now, here's the beauty of realizing that only the *spiritual energy of this Universe* defines you. Once you make the conscious discovery that I AM the divine energy of this *Universe*; I AM the sacred energy of *Love;* And I AM the energy of everlasting *Life,* only then will it become inconceivable for any man-made logo to dictate who you are; because once you awaken to the reality of what really defines you it becomes impossible for any man-made label to stick to what is *intangible.*

On a much deeper level, we are all unique conscious Beings of this Universe, 'consciously' experiencing other unique forms of life. And if we human beings do not awaken and escape our subconscious minds and realize that this Universe in its *'entirety' does not and will not ever* **exclusively** reside only within one image described by man, then our paradigms will continue to rule and belittle us by making us *subconscious* servants.

As long as we human beings continue to oblige the man-made idea that this Universe appears in the form of an omnipotent and <u>*oppressive*</u> man that we should all *surrender* to and fear, then we will never be free to experience *Heaven on Earth;* because we will always be a slave to man's *manipulating* notion of this Universe. Hence, we will never be able to see another human being as we see our *'selves'*, considering our man-made *'selves'* are a byproduct of many *different* and *divisive* man-made concepts that limits this possibility.

Therefore, the only way we will ever be able to *see* another human being as we *see* our *'selves'* is through discovering 'insight', which will allow us to become more 'insightful' that the energy from this vast Universe lives within all humanity. And through this *enlightening lens*, it will become *crystal clear* that it is only the conscious energy that stems from 'One' divine Universe that is a true reflection of one's *divine self*.

So I ask you, how can we ever expect to have a true loving relationship with this Universe and the rest of humanity if our religions <u>*make us believe*</u> that we human beings are not one with this Universe or innately connected to each other?

Please know beyond our *disruptive* religious conviction, every form of conscious life on this planet is <u>one</u> with this **<u>One</u>** divine Universe.

Now as this chapter comes to an end, the European and Middle Eastern 'male' theory surrounding this Universe must also come to an end, considering if it does not, then this self-controlling belief will lead to our self-destruction.

Chapter VI

This self-destructive prophecy has been proven evident as far back as the War of the Crusades, when a Christian army went to war against Muslim forces and a countless number of souls sacrificed and lost their lives defending and honoring irrational ideas of this Universe. Although, if we took the time and made a conscious effort to think about the different man-made identities of this Universe, we would come to know that they are extremely childish and impractical. Believing that this Universe is defined by 'Love' is one thing; however, desperately needing to believe that this Universe is defined by 'only' one 'Man' is a farfetched story.

With all this being said, let's face it, no human being will ever be qualified to 'physically' identify who or what represents this Universe, because the vast 'hidden' nature of this Universe is not physical, which of course makes 'worshipping' any 'male' idea of this Universe as a symbol of truth, is in reality, honoring an improbability.

See every religious believer is under the impression that they are merely supporting their belief or their idea, which they themselves possess; not once realizing that this belief or idea actually possesses them.

I do realize this book speaks to my personal theory of this Universe. However, please know that I am not asking anyone to believe a word that I say. All I ask is that you 'feel' the message within this material and allow my theory to speak for itself.

Thus, whether it's my theory or someone else's; in my opinion the most 'loving' and 'rational' theory of this Universe should win.

VII

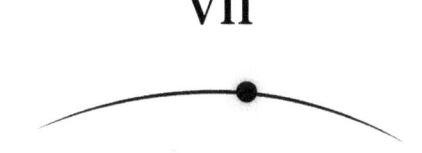

The Pursuit of Wholeness

Do you know, although religion tries to uplift us; in reality it puts us down?

Do you know that every man-made religion profits off of our/ its beliefs?

Do you know that there is no man-made religion that can actually help save 'us' from our 'selves'?

I know the Christian Bible states that every human being is in the pursuit of "Holiness", which is the state of being sanctified or blessed. In other words, it is the divine state of being *Godly!*

Well, of course the word Holiness doesn't exist outside of the Holy Bible. Therefore, I am going to translate the word Holy, into *Wholly*. Because once we become *Whole* with the divine energy of this Universe, our pursuit for Holiness or *Wholeness* is over.

<u>*Here is what I mean*</u>:

In my opinion, *once we, **the soul** observer, become aware of our divine nature,* this conscious discovery will be the conclusion to: *"The Pursuit of Holiness" or "The Pursuit of Wholeness."* See, we can never become holy or whole until we recognize what *solely* defines us. In other words, if we continue to listen to our man-made selves, we will remain *un-wholly* human beings.

Thus, the *marriage* that we have formed with our selves has in turn *divorced* our awareness from who we really are.

According to the Bible, God says to the Israelites in the wilderness, "Be holy as I am holy" (I Peter 1:16) which translates to me as saying:

Once our awareness becomes whole or *one* with our true nature, then as I mentioned above, our pursuit for holiness or wholeness is over. Since through this awareness, we will have finally envisioned the nature of what it is like to actually be universal. In other words, until we, as souls observers, become aware that we are indeed the awareness of this Universe in human form; we will remain *broken* because the soul of who we are is not in proper alignment or in harmony with itself.

Hence, in order to be in concert with this Universe, the *subconscious mind, body, and soul* must be in harmony. Notice how all three of these entities *stand alone.* However, as it stands now our lives are in disharmony because we as *universal souls* are technically not in accord with our own lives.

The main reason I prefer to use the word *Wholly* is because at birth every human being is born unbroken, complete, or *whole.* This means no human being was born of this earth *emotionally scared.* Therefore, during our infant years we live in accordance with our true loving nature and exude a *loving feeling* for genuine life.

<u>Here's an example of what I mean</u>:

Jesus called a little child to come to him. Jesus stood the child before the followers. Then Jesus said, "I tell you the truth. You must change and become like little children [in your hearts]. If you don't do this, you will never enter the kingdom of heaven. The greatest [most important] person in the kingdom of heaven is the person that makes himself humble like this child" (Matthew 18:2–4 KJV).

At the beginning of early childhood, we see the true wonder of life in a child's eyes. Life during this time is fascinating and intriguing. Observe how infants interact with their immediate surroundings; *no judgment, no hatred, no fears, or worries.* What we are witnessing is more than infants engaging with their physical environment. It is young conscious Beings exuding undistracted awareness and bonding with life as it exists within the present moment.

Notice how we are more conscious and aware as infants, than we are as adults. In truth, as an infant, we know more about *official life*, than we do as an adult. Considering, as an adult we have grown to know only a 'conceptual' idea of life. Precious life during these early moments is a magnificent blessing. This is when *a young conscious observer* is experiencing other *life* forms of itself, in its *purest essence, as an undiminished human being.*

Then out of the shadow of the darkness an assault takes place. Man's ego begins to creep into the *light* of a child's consciousness, and places a blanket over the young soul's awareness which ultimately blinds a soul from official life. Thus, it is not until man's ego distorts a young Being's awareness through injecting man-made ideas and theories into a vulnerable child's mind that we proceed to lose the curiosity for authentic life.

Also during this early stage of existence, we are not distracted from the present moment because our subconscious mind has yet to become *completely* polluted with man-made beliefs that *lie about our past* and makes us *fear and worry about our future.* But, as our subconscious mind becomes infected with man-made rhetoric, this slowly proceeds to sever our awareness from our divine essence of *Being*. And unfortunately, this is when we begin to think that our human forms are what define us; which is when we cease being *Wholly* as human beings and begin to live our lives in the *broken form* of being *only human.*

And once the soul of who we are begins to merge with a man-made concept of itself, the essence of who we are becomes smothered and our true identity becomes concealed for a lifetime. Hence, this is when we begin to believe that our man-made *'self'* defines us; which is when we all become *"lost souls."*

Do you ever wonder where the joy for life ends and suffering begins?

I want you to think back to when you stopped enjoying life and you began worrying about it. In other words, I want you to make a sincere attempt to tap into when your joy for life proceeded to migrate toward suffering through life.

Now, if you have made a sincere effort toward exploring this inquiry you will notice that the transition from joy to suffering begins to happen as we start to **change** over from childhood into adulthood.

You see, at an early age, we are taught to believe in certain man-made concepts. However, at this stage of development, these concepts have yet to become fastened permanently to our paradigm. This means we have yet to *wholeheartedly* accept and comply with these man-made concepts as being who we are. In other words, at this impressionable age, we have not been completely sold on man's false impression of *Self, Life, and God.* Therefore, these man-made convictions have yet to be proven guilty for our offensive behavior.

However, as we approach our teenage years and then crossover into adulthood, these man-made concepts eventually become etched into our psyche. And once these man-made concepts are ingrained into our paradigm we begin to defend and protect them because we believe they define us. Thus, the fonder we become of man's *divisive* and *destructive* concepts of Self, Life, and God, the more our precious life begins to transform into a "Living Hell!"

Did you know the soulful essence of our 'Being' is the most essential part of being a human being?

We are all born as pure and divine human beings. Over time our man-made conditioning proceeds to separate us from our true nature of *Being*. After our ego begins to establish itself within our subconscious minds it then proceeds to *erase* our *awareness* of Being. And this Being which defines us is the most pivotal and crucial ingredient within every human *being*. Nonetheless, due to our inability to be able to control our awareness, our ego has been able to download a *Selfish Human Virus* into our subconscious mind. And this mind filled disease has created a 'dis-ease' in humanity and has convinced us that no one will own the right to offend our *human image*.

This *Being* which represents us, can also be classified as the soul, and as a *conscious soul* we are connected to this Universe, and also to one another. Hence, this *Being* is the inherent, unchanging, *'conscious'* nature of a Human *Being*.

See, as we aimlessly maneuver through life with no real direction we have been conditioned to believe that this approach towards life is ordinary. When in truth there is nothing natural about the way we live. We all *methodically* live our lives conforming to a man-made standard that everyone else subconsciously lives by. Therefore, we don't truly live, we only exist.

In other words, there is nothing reasonable about the way we *act* or *behave*. Until we discern this knowing for our *'selves'* we will continue to comply with a man-made concept that fraudulently defines our personal identity.

Chapter VII

Here's an example of what I mean:

If you physically appear a certain way and you do not obey the man-made concept that outlines your physical image, well, some individuals will proclaim that you are a *sellout,* or ask the following question: "Why are you *acting* like someone else?"

When in reality no matter what *racial concept* we are obliging we are all *performing* incongruently to our true nature.

Speaking of our true nature, do you know that we human beings are one with nature? Or better yet, a 'soul' part of this divine Universe?

In my opinion, I sense we human beings have no idea that we are one with nature, and more to the point, we are an intricate part of nature itself! Quite frankly, I feel that we human beings believe that we are above all forms of *nature.* So, allow me to ask you this, "Do you realize through believing that the Universe *only* lives within the *male form* of Jesus, Allah, Buddha, Jehovah, etc., you are in essence diminishing the vast universal nature of this Universe?"

See, we human beings must try to understand that the energy of this Universe is represented within all forms of conscious life. This means this Universe lives within all forms of nature, hence the expression *"God lives everywhere."*

However, since our paradigms have persuaded us to believe that we human beings are above all fashions of nature we are declaring that our *human flesh* is above this divine Universe. In other words, we are *confessing* that our material image is more precious and sacred than the conscious energy of *life itself.*

Therefore, please try to comprehend the following statement because it is very important.

When we human beings are praying to our religious version of this Universe, we are only worshipping the *human image of man versus addressing the 'Soul' nature of this Universe.* This is why we human beings show no real love or respect for *Father Sun* or Mother Earth and our religious leaders want it to remain this way. Since the less we know about our *true nature*, the more *control* our man-made religions have over our misguided lives. Therefore, since we have no Earthly idea that we are a *sophisticated* part of this Universe, we are in disharmony with all forms of nature. This is probably why *Mother Nature* expresses her anger in the form of *Natural Disasters*.

In reality, we all need to awaken to our true nature and show Father Sun and Mother Earth more love and respect. Peace on Earth can only be achieved through the divine nature of love and harmony. If we continue to choose not to be in harmony with nature, then Mother Nature or Mother Earth will eventually destroy us, before we ever destroy her.

Do you know the mystery of life lives within all forms of nature?

If we really think we need to believe in something, then we need to make a valid effort towards believing that we are more than who we *think* we are.

What I have come to realize is that our human suffering is a result of our frustration with an *artificial existence* that our paradigms have created, and this in turn has developed this *Mystery of the Human Unknown*. In a nutshell, our human resentment is over what we *subconsciously think* life is.

In order for us human beings to be free from our human affliction we must be liberated from who we think we are. Since, this man-made concept of who we think we are is what's preserving the mystery of the human unknown.

See, we human beings must understand how to control our awareness in order to look beyond what we physically see and envision the *true miracle of life* that lives within every living form of nature. Once the essence of our true nature begins to consciously resonate, the mystery of the human unknown will then reveal itself to our subconscious mind.

<u>This means when we plug into our divine internal light this shift in awareness will cast clarity upon the true meaning of life. And once the true nature of life resonates with our subconscious mind, our physical forms that contain the "conscious energy of life" will begin to 'visibly' melt away. Thus, the seen will become unseen, and it will then become apparent that it is only the divine essence of life itself that really matters.</u> However, we must be patient with this process because we have been struggling with this human mystery for centuries. Therefore, unveiling this ancient mystery will be based upon how much of our bulletproof self-image we will need to blast through in order to consciously encounter the truth.

Since we human beings believe that our human images exemplify who we are, this attachment to what is not true, equates to our malfunction. Thus, our failure to know the truth not only facilitates our *fake sense of 'self'*, it also manifests a *false feeling for life*. And because our paradigms constantly steer us away from the true nature of this Universe, we are ignorant of the sacred truth that represents who we are.

Here is what I find to be ironic. We human beings believe that out of all universal creations we have been chosen to *control* and *rule* the world. However, out of all creations we human beings are the most *out of control* and *unruly* creatures on the planet.

Every other living species behaves according to their true Universal nature. Every insect and animal (with the exception of the human animal) on our planet is aware of life as it was designed to be. We human beings are the only living species in this realm of reality that do not *consciously* experience life through our true nature. Therefore, everything we *subconsciously think* we know about life is, in truth, a *man-made lie!*

<u>*Why? You may ask:*</u>

Well, because our beliefs have pulled the wool over our awareness; which in turn has blinded us from being aware of true reality.

See, we live within the irrationality of our subconscious mind, tucked away in a dreary back room steadily watching re-runs of how horrible our life seems to be, because our ego is *remotely controlling* our lives through *religiously* replaying our deepest darkest thoughts. Please understand, we will only be able to recognize the *light* of day once the true loving nature of who we are *shines* within our subconscious mind. Upon this enlightening revelation, brightness will drive out the darkness. And as it has been said, *"Darkness cannot live in the presence of light."* Thus, we human beings must attempt to acknowledge that our authentic nature as sacred human beings is to live life in the presence of reality, which will in turn create Peace, Love, and Harmony.

Since our paradigms have been able to successfully conceal our true loving nature, we live our lives only in the dissembled form of *Being* only human. This results in the *synthetic* human nature of *Being restless, hateful, fearful, and depressed.* Hence, under our man-made conditioning, we tread through life confused.

For the majority of our lives, we have cherished the man-made belief that our self-images define who we are. And through this false perception of self we have *lost full sight* of our divine nature. As the popular saying goes *"Out of sight, out of mind."*

So, let's expand upon how we become lost souls?

Shortly after we are born of this world as undiminished human beings our man-made beliefs, which conflict with our true nature, begin to invade our subconscious minds. And by way of this invasion, the divine essence of who we are is hijacked.

As young souls we are defenseless between the elementary ages of one through five. During this inaugural stage of life we do not have the rational capacity to govern what enters into our subconscious minds. Hence, these man-made controlling beliefs now have an advantage because our sub conscious minds are not being *rationally* guarded. Therefore, they are now completely exposed to *questionable* and *irrational* beliefs.

We rely on our loved ones and people we trust such as our Parents, Teachers, Pastors, or Preachers, etc., to construct a proper foundation for us. This foundation would then be leveraged to support prosperity in our lives.

Despite what we have been conditioned to believe, prosperity has absolutely nothing to do with flourishing financially, but it has everything to do with how *well our feelings flourish*. Hence, living a prosperous life has *everything* to do with the nature of *one's well Being*. Therefore, the more we are embellished with the *'feelings'* of peace, love, and joy the more our lives are filled with prosperity.

In addition to the false perception of financial prosperity, we are also taught to believe that it is our *man-made concept of race*, as well as, our *man-made cultures* that define us. And it is these *imprecise* building blocks which are used to form our reality that actually create an unstable infrastructure.

Unfortunately, since our parents know no better, they continue to recycle these *manipulating* man-made concepts that they were exposed to; thus our man-made egos lives on. This egoist conditioning has plagued humanity for eons.

In summary, here's an example of what defines a lost soul.

The *soul* of who we are is *lost* within the plethora of *man-made beliefs* that are circulating and *lying* deep within the parameters of our subconscious mind.

Now, let's address how our paradigms distract us from our true nature.

As I mentioned above, it all starts with our man-made conditioning going back to when we were toddlers. Every form of what we are taught to believe begins to construct an insecure *sub-structure* within our *subconscious mind* for who we think we are. This incapacitated thinking not only separates us from one another but it also detaches our thoughts from who we are. Hence, our detachment from who we are, attaches us to the ill nature of our *man-made paradigms* which are responsible for manifesting our human failures.

Therefore, it is our *uncontrolled conscious thinking*, which is the main cause of all of our human problems; considering our awareness is constantly being misplaced. And this conscious disunion from the truth makes it easy for our ego to *control* and draw our attention towards the bogus data that has been stored within our subconscious minds.

As I mentioned in a previous chapter, our paradigms alone are responsible for constructing this *unawareness of official life* by way of vacuuming our attention into a past and future vortex. This makes it difficult for us to engage in life that lives within the present moment.

Translation: *The majority of our thoughts relate to our past problems and future worries; which makes us oblivious to the peaceful present.*

Therefore, we must understand that what we believe to be true about our *'selves'* is not based upon the validity of the information. It is based more upon the unscrupulous conditioning to make the *man-made* information appear to be valid.

Okay, I have a 'soulful' question for you. If we declare that we have a soul, then what role do we believe our soul plays, as it relates to our reality? In other words, if we believe that we have a soul, then why do we view our soul so metaphorically?

Chapter VII

The main reason we human beings refer to the soul so metaphorically and struggle with the notion of actually being **THE** soul is because our souls are not tangible. This translates to "If the soul is not physically evident, then how can it be relevant to my physical reality?" And since we cannot physically identify with the soul, we do not dignify our *'selves'* as being souls; which is why we human beings live an inappropriate human life.

See, until we as *the soul observer* spiritually sense the true energy of who we are we will continue to believe that our human form is what naturally defines us. This means *we* as *souls* will forever be cornered within the demeaning maze of our own subconscious minds.

What I find interesting is we human beings often claim to *have souls*. Well, whether we realize this or not, if we declare that we have souls then we are actually declaring that our human flesh defines us. Unfortunately this means if we believe that our *man-made image* represents who we are then we as souls will continue to suffer because we have chosen to worship a man-made concept of who we think we are.

Now, allow me to ask you a very important question. "Do you believe Jesus' Holy Mission was based upon a 'selfish' assignment"? Do you believe that Jesus' loving desire for us to pursue Holiness or 'Wholeness' was strictly 'self' centered?

I know Christianity wants us to believe that Jesus Christ is simultaneously both *The God who created and rules this Universe,* as well as *The 'Son'* of this Universe within the human flesh. And as we are expected to believe in this man-made concept, we are also forced to fear and believe that no other human being bears the impression of this Universe.

Although, for the most part I do believe religion was established with good intentions. However, when our religions make us believe that the divinity of this entire Universe resides only in one 'male' image, this belief itself is what robs every religious believer of their divine birthright. Or in other words, when we honor the religious belief that only one individual image is worthy of sacredness, this belief in turn strips every religious being of their universal divinity.

Nonetheless, I must admit, I do feel that an *enlightened* being that we call Jesus did exist and walked this Earth in human form. And in the same breath, I do not feel that the life story of Jesus is accurately depicted within *man's bible*.

See, what I have discovered is that we are all the essence or 'conscious energy' of this divine Universe; and we are also the *'Sun of God'* within the human flesh, which I will further expand upon in the following chapter.

The colossal difference between Jesus and most of humanity is that Jesus was a *highly enlightened* human being who possessed *"Christ"* or in other words, *"Anointed Consciousness,"* which means Jesus was *consciously aware* that he was the *Sun of God*—by way of the universal *energy of life*—that was bestowed upon him through *Father Sun*.

We human beings have lost true *awareness* of the *light* that defines us. Thus, this makes us highly *'unenlightened'* human beings, since we can't seem to consciously conceptualize that we are a reflection of the *'Sun' of the Universe*.

Unfortunately, we human beings will forever believe in man's concept of a *Universal Ruler* until we awaken to realize that *'Love'* is the one and only *Universal Rule* that we all need to live by.

Please allow me to say this; I do feel that based upon humanity's current bewildered state of man-made conditioning, Christianity and the Good Book do serve as a good moral compass. However, it's the moral of the Jesus story that leaves me with a lot of doubt.

I feel the Biblical story surrounding the resurrection of Jesus Christ does not serve to save the lives of humanity; I sense the

Jesus story was formed only to *sustain the life of Christianity*. It is only our man-made belief pertaining to this questionable fable that helps keep this mythical story alive.

See, I personally sense that Jesus' Holy Mission was to share the *conscious truth,* eventually, with all humankind that we all share the *Sun of this Universe,* and once we recognize this as being the *sole/soul* truth, this is when we will finally become Holy—or in other words *whole* with our true nature. This means we will cease existing in the dysfunctional form of **Being** *only human* and start living more *Wholly* as loving human beings. Upon this *enlightening* discovery, our *Beings* will at last be *born again.* And our human forms will then be restored or in other words *resurrected,* and *salvation* will be bestowed upon the souls of all humanity.

So, what is the true Gospel of 'Being' Reborn?

If we believe that through Jesus' assumed sacrifice for our human sins we are considered to be reborn, and thus Jesus *supposedly* saved us, then why are we still suffering? In my opinion, in order to be rescued from our *'selves'* we must *'will'* our *'selves'* to know that our human image does not hold priority over us—*the souls of this Universe.*

Until humanity acknowledges this as the Gospel, we will continue to *'subconsciously'* exist in this man-made world, through dwelling on the mystery of the human unknown, along with being scared and confused as it relates to the perplexity of what man calls life.

This man-made abuse will be prolonged as long as the core Universal energy of who we are remains *consciously dead* to us.

If humanity continues to drift through life believing that we are *only* human and never become aware that we are the soul, then we will never behold the true meaning of life. We will always resemble the walking dead, until we awaken to the truth that needs our attention.

See, only through a *Beings conscious rebirth* will we ever be reborn and until then humanity will always be scorned.

Now, here is my perception of what Jesus meant in terms of (Being) born again:

"**I**", the untouchable *Being,* which is the conscious energy that grants *sacred life* into my human form, was born again due to my conscious awareness of my own divine nature. In other words, we must become aware that we are indeed the <u>*conscious Being*</u> that our *man-made ego* laid to rest years ago, by way of masking our awareness. This *Being* is the authentic blueprint that ***solely exemplifies*** who we are. Once this enlightening information is plugged into our subconscious mind, this newfound awareness will bring *new life* back into our true essence of *Being*. Hence, the divine energy of *who we are* has now been *born again.*

Please note any illustration pertaining to 'Being' and 'Soul' are referencing the same sacred energy.

So, here is my interpretation of Jesus' mission for us to pursue Wholeness:

Jesus' Holy *Wholly* mission was to try to get us, *the souls of this Universe,* to become whole with our divine nature by discerning that we as universal souls is the *light* which shines bright within our human form. Then, and only then, will *we* as universal *souls,* proceed to exit the darkness of our subconscious minds and enter into the *conscious light of reality.*

So, in light of the above information, do you really believe that the only way we will ever enter into the Kingdom of Heaven is through accepting Jesus Christ as our Lord and Savior? Which in turn means, if we do not accept Jesus as our personal Savior, then we will not be allowed to enter into 'His' Kingdom and there will be no exceptions!

Chapter VII

Now, according to the Christian religion we are conditioned to believe that this world we *presently* live in is Hell. And the only way to enter into a sacred domain that man calls Heaven is to accept Jesus Christ as our Lord and Savior. However, if we choose not to accept Jesus as our *religious Redeemer*, then he will not accept us. And, unfortunately, it does not matter how *loving* of a human being you are. Consider this, if you do not satisfy Jesus' demands, then you will not be welcomed into his Heavenly Kingdom. Hence, the soul of who you are has just earned a one way trip to Hell. In my humble opinion, this simply does not make any *sacred* sense, which in turn makes me "sense" that this is just another reflection of man's nonsense.

Therefore, do you really believe that there is actually a "Man upstairs" and if so, why?

Whether this is a figure of speech or not, this question begs to be addressed. This man-made expression tends to create a false sense of reality which constructs an illusion that there is actually a stairway to Heaven that leads to one *Supreme Man* that we should all *fear and worship*.

See, Man's portrayal of this Universe is simply a portrait of him *'self'*. Hence, if you notice as it pertains to most religions, this Universe is never represented in the beautiful form of a woman. This Universe is always in the barbaric form of one common **denominator**—*A Male Chauvinist!* This sexist *man-made* idea that a woman was created from the rib of man indeed says it all.

<u>With this being said, let's take this moment to honor a woman's true nature:</u>

A woman's life is generally conducted by how she *feels* and a man's life is governed by what he *thinks*. See, man's self-destructive paradigm has him confused in terms of what real strength is. The male *ego* has persuaded modern man that any manifestation of *love* or any display of *your divine nature* is a sign of weakness. This is why some men perceive women as being weak, and their man-made perspective of a woman's feelings are not important. What men fail to recognize is that exhibiting love is what makes us human beings so unique and extraordinary.

Therefore, if you choose not to honor what truly defines your *universal* nature, then you have chosen to redefine your *'self'* as being less than human. This may explain why some men are so barbaric and *inhumane.*

In ages past, women were revered as *Goddesses* because they are the ones who physically give birth to *new generations.* Each stage of a woman's life was viewed as a critical crossroad, or rite of passage. Women understand cycles because they serve as the *incubators of life,* and there is an intrinsic ebb and flow to the feminine experience. Each monthly cycle of an adult woman's life, forms a complete cycle of birth and death; this is a microcosm of the *physical form* itself.

Like life itself, a woman's expressions can be alternately gentle, fierce, loving, and nurturing. Feminine power is *magnetic and attractive,* unlike *superficial masculine power* which is an egoist program established within the subconscious mind of a man that activates a false sense of power, which makes a man think he needs to conquer and claim whatever he wants.

The power of a woman is also like the all-encompassing *depths* of the ocean—able to consume all the sorrows within this man-made world, yet still have the *deep loving soul* to give. Hence, I realize women are not only the bearers of life; they are also the bearers of love.

Therefore, in the name of *Almighty Love,* let's extract the essence of a woman from life as we know it today. Let's say this precious gift that we call a woman was never granted upon man. If a woman never existed, this world would be the most heinous and unbearable place to live.

Chapter VII

Imagine this planet under the total influence of *out of control male egos,* recklessly roaming and governing this realm of reality. Now try to *envision* this world existing without the *loving soul of women.* I am sure once you conceptualize this situation you will foresee "*Hell on Earth."*

Okay, with all this being stated, let's refer back to the egoist nature of man. Ironically each religious God constructed in *man's self-image,* not only appears to be extremely insecure, but also outrageously *selfish,* with an ego the size of King Kong.

I find it very interesting that our religions force us to believe that our present realm of reality is Hell, when Hell only resides within our paradigms which are manifestations of murky beliefs stored in our subconscious minds. Thus, it is the *man-made lies* that we all live by within the dark dimensions of our subconscious minds that tends to spill over into the present moment that *makes us believe* this glorious planet is Hell on Earth.

See, as it pertains to this Earthly realm of reality, we as souls of this Universe are on trial to consciously discover who we are. Therefore, if we fail to recognize our true nature and the energy of this divine Universe that lives within every precious moment of life, then what makes us believe that we will *graduate* with *honors* to the next Heavenly level simply by accepting man's religious version of this Universe as our Savior?

Please allow me to ask you a delicate question: Do you really believe that Jesus died on a cross for our sins?

Well, in my opinion, I find it very difficult to believe that Jesus actually died on a cross to save us from our sins.

<u>And why you may ask</u>?

Well, because our sins have gotten horribly worse!

If Jesus really sacrificed his life on a cross to save us from our sins, then wouldn't this logically mean that our *man-made sins* would be extinguished? And considering our sins are still running rampant, please help me to understand why this Universe would send his only begotten Son to place His life on the line, or on a cross, to save humanity from a horrendous condition that is still a human infestation?

Well if you ask me, Jesus did not give his life to 'save' us from our sins; his life was taken as a byproduct of the man-made sins that we 'save' and then act upon within our subconscious minds. See, what I find interesting is Jesus, the *'enlightened'* human being, has absolutely nothing to do with this Christian God concept; it is only man him *'self'* who has conditioned us to believe that Jesus is the divine Deity of this Universe.

So, speaking of our sins, allow me to ask you this question: Do you feel that our 'life' may be far more divine than the way it has been 'religiously' defined within our subconscious mind?

Please know that our lives are far more valuable than we *religiously* think.

What I find really bothersome is how some religious propaganda preaches to the contrary. This destructive dogma works hard towards convincing us that per our true nature we are all born and destined to be sinners. However, what I find even more disturbing is how we still feel obligated to worship and hand over our lives to our religions that deem us human beings as *Being* worthless.

We need to cease believing that by our true nature we are born to be sinners. Since, by our genuine nature, we are all born as *untainted loving* children of this Universe.

Therefore, for our own sake, we need to stop believing that this Universe, created us to live a life of *fear, hatred, greed, envy, etc.* If we think about this *man-made* notion it screams of being ridiculous.

Chapter VII

In reality *sin* is a condition that is man-made. Our societies are dedicated towards ensuring that all of humanity is conditioned to be sinners; we have all been *tainted* to view each other in a disgraceful way. And despite what we are conditioned to believe, religion is in no way the overall truth; it is only a temporary Band-Aid, which is used to aid in our current man-made suffering. And this religious Band-Aid that we human beings have been wearing for centuries does not heal us; considering that beneath the surface of what we have been taught to believe we are all still emotionally scared.

Do you know only the truth will set us free and only the truth will provide us with real fulfillment? Therefore, with this being asked, I ask you this crucial question, "Do you truly believe our religion(s) provide us with a true sense of freedom and fulfillment?"

Well, if your answer is yes, then as the saying goes. God Bless you!

Thus, if *we* are honest with our *'self'*, we will instinctively feel that our religions leave us somewhat *empty;* considering in reality, our religions are not *filling* us with the **whole** truth.

See, our elected religions work overtime to teach us that they are a perfect reflection of the sacred truth. However, please understand that the sacred truth can never be taught; it can only be encountered. And this discovery can only be unlocked once we discern that we possess the key to all we seek. Thus, until we awaken from this man-made spell and acknowledge that we are all born and instilled with the sacred truth, this unawareness will forever make us a *convict* to our religious *convictions*.

Please understand humanity will always suffer and be scorned until we reveal our internal truth. In a nutshell, we will never envision the sacred energy of who we are as long as we remain baffled by our religious beliefs.

Therefore, please know if a religious document supposedly bears the ultimate truth, then explain to me why the truth is *misinterpreted* in a million different ways. Hence, the bona fide truth is defined by an *actual state of reality.* Thus, the truth is something that is *verified* and *undisputable* and would never be so puzzling to comprehend.

Therefore in truth, *beneath the physical surface of whom we think we are, we human beings are composed of atoms and energy. Hence, we human beings are the divine 'conscious energy' of this Universe that physically experiences life through our human forms!*

Therefore, the only way we will ever experience the energy of this Universe, is through *feeling* **ITS** spiritual power. Thus, if we continue to *believe* that we will one day physically see our man-made concept of this Universe, then we will never experience the true divine nature of this Universe.

In other words, though we may believe that we will one day *feast our eyes* on our religious version of this Universe, in *reality,* this will never come to fruition considering, in *reality,* it is virtually impossible to bear witness to the *intangible energy of love.*

Please know, as long as we continue to believe in unproven religious stories, our life's journey will end well before it ever begins.

The following Biblical passage is a perfect example of how Jesus' mission was to help man save the soul of who they are from their man-made sense of 'self'. Jesus' Holy 'wholly' mission is over, now it is time for our journey to commence, in order to discover the 'eternal truth' that will free us from our 'selves'.

Gaining the World; Losing Your Soul

Then calling the crowd to join his disciples he said; "If any of you want to be my follower, you must turn from your *selfish* ways, *take up your cross,* and follow me. If you try to hang on to your life, you will lose it. But if you give up your life for my sake and for the sake of the Good News, you will save it (Matthew 10:38–39).

And what do you benefit if you gain the whole world but lose your own soul? Is anything worth more than your soul?" (Matthew 16:26).

Let me ask you a question: What is your interpretation of "take up your cross?"

Here's my interpretation:

Jesus said you must turn from your *selfish* ways, '*take up your cross*', and follow me. Well in my opinion we must first relinquish our man-made sense of *'self'* that falsely defines *us*. And then do away with our *religious cross* that manifests our *fears and worries* which in turn bears our pain, and then follow Jesus to discover the *eternal truth* that resides within our human form.

See, in my opinion, Jesus' Holy *Wholly* mission was pioneered to help save us from our *man-made sense of self* via acknowledging that the only way we will ever be saved or in other words be rescued from our subconscious mind, is through the process of cleansing our awareness. This means, as souls of this Universe, we must extinguish our man-made sense of self, as well as eliminate from our subconscious minds the ingrained belief that we have formed for our man-made concept of this Universe.

I know for some, the following statement will be difficult to accept. However, simply accepting Jesus Christ as our Lord and Savior will not *save us* from what we ultimately suffer.

Religion is really a form of medication.

In other words, religion is a prescription that has been prescribed only to ease our pain. But, no matter how much of our religious rhetoric we consume there will never be a dosage strong enough to ultimately *heal* what we *internally suffer* from. Hence, despite our religious conditioning, please understand one thing; *we* can only save *who we 'really' are* from our *selves*.

Therefore, we need to try to open our subconscious mind to the reality that the true essence of this Universe will only help us if we make a valid attempt to separate *who we are* from our *'self'*. Thus, as it has been said, *"God can only help those who help them 'selves'."*

The whole purpose of this information is to warn us to be careful of the *religious* nourishment that we're being fed; considering it may not be for our own *spiritual* good.

However, after it is all said and done, whether we discern this or not, the choice that we make might not be our own. Just make certain that your *'religious ego'* is not making this life staking decision for you.

So, the bottom line is we can continue to worship Man's *'Divisive'* concept of Religion or pursue *'Wholeness'* through Spiritual Peace.

With this being stated, do you know what the fundamental difference is between Spirituality and Religion?

The fundamental difference between Spirituality and Religion is that Religion *forces* us into believing in its version of this Universe, whereas, Spirituality allows us to experience the true nature of this Universe *naturally. Thus, Religion is about worship, whereas Spirituality is about relationship.*

Now, here is the *monumental* difference between Spirituality and Religion. Spirituality provides us with a *peace* of subconscious mind that will manifest into *peace* on Earth; whereas Religion demands a *piece* of our subconscious mind, which creates Hell on Earth. Therefore, if you haven't notice lately, Hell is what we are all experiencing on a **subconscious** level.

Chapter VII

Nevertheless, we are conditioned to believe that religion is the one and only solution to our man-made problems. However, once we awaken to what really defines us we will discover how religion is not the remedy to our problems. In reality, religion is what actually gives birth to all of our *fears* and *worries.*

Although religion attempts to teach us good moral values via religious scripture—unfortunately, it's the undying love that we have formed for our man-made version of this Universe that has formulated our human hardship. Therefore, there is *no time like the present* to relinquish our childhood beliefs and commence to vacate our religious nest and spread our wings and soar through life—not as *broken* humans, but as restored *Wholly* human beings.

Please know that we are all children of this Universe, who are created for one *sole/soul* purpose; and that is to *consciously love* one another. I know this is difficult to envision considering we all live such judgmental lives. However, please understand that the universal energy of who we are is born before the *man-made development* of who we think we are is *formed.*

In other words, our essential lives as *eternal conscious 'Beings'* are present, before any man-made belief *matters*. Hence, our birth as conscious *Beings* is what grants *sacred life* to our human form.

So, I sincerely ask you this question; "Why do we choose to be <u>solely</u> human, when we are 'souly' so much more?"

VIII

God's Immortal Soul (Sol)

Okay, as we have reached this point, I have a question for you, "Do you now sense that the soul or spirit of this Universe may authentically define us? Or do you still believe that we are separate from what we consider to be our soul?"

What I am really asking is, "Do you still believe it is only our 'human flesh' that defines us and not necessarily the soul of this Universe?"

And with this being said, do you believe animals or any other non-human life form is represented by the soul of this Universe?

Well, as you proceed to marinate upon the above list of questions, allow me to interrupt and address the concept of what most human beings deem as being the *human soul*.

Many religious, philosophical, psychological, and mythological traditions view the soul as being the incorporeal and immortal *essence* of a person, living thing, or object. However, according to some religions, the *human soul* is the only soul capable of union with the divine.

The most common synonyms associated with the human soul are: *spirit, mind, psyche, and self.* Some eastern religions even believe that our egos define the human soul.

Chapter VIII

Now, although there may be somewhat of a current connection between our egos and the soul, I personally know that we as souls of this Universe were not born with an ego. We developed this man-made monster through traveling along the dark and desolate roads within our subconscious minds while being mugged by man-made beliefs.

<u>*So, with all this being said, here is my perception of the human soul*</u>:

There is only one thing that defines all *living Beings* and that is the *soul of this Universe.*

We human beings are not the only living species in this Universe that is privileged with *'Being'*—an immortal soul. The synonyms I prefer to use to represent the incorporeal soul are: *consciousness, life, Being, energy, spirit, the* **light,** and last but not least; the *power of love*.

Now, before I completely reveal my vision of **THE** immortal soul of this Universe, please know the primary purpose of this chapter is to construct enough *rational insight* so that the *light* will be able to shine upon the soul of who we are and bestow upon us genuine enlightenment.

Okay, let's get started. I am going to begin by comparing how our physical composition is a direct reflection of the composition of the *Sun of this Universe or in other words the Sun of God*. First I am going to list the atomic abundance of the Sun's most common elements beginning with **Hydrogen** which is 91.2% and then I will proceed with the following elements in order:

- Helium (8.7%)
- Oxygen (.078%)
- Carbon (.043%)
- Iron (.030%)

- Sulfur (.015%)
- Nitrogen (.0088%)
- Magnesium (.0038%)

So how does the Sun produce energy?

<u>Here is a general answer</u>:

The Sun produces energy by the nuclear fusion of hydrogen into helium in its core. What this means is that at the core's high temperature and pressure the hydrogen atoms fuse into helium atoms. In this reaction about 0.8% of the hydrogen mass is converted into energy. The energy from this exothermic reaction is eventually transferred from the core by radiation and convection to the surface (photosphere) from which it is radiated out into space as electromagnetic radiation, mostly in the visible and infrared wavelengths.

The Earth's atmosphere filters out and reflects some of the Sun's rays and passes the remainder to the Earth's surface. This is called the Earth's surface insolation. The word *Sol*, which originates from the name ***Solar***, is the Latin name for Sun. This is how the Earth's surface is heated, but then it is lost again every night—radiated out into the cold darkness of space. And of course, without *the Sun there would be little if any life on* the Earth.

Most forms of life use solar energy in many ways. Plants use photosynthesis to convert light into chemical energy (carbohydrates). The chemical energy stored within plants, in turn feeds most living things on Earth. When we eat food made from plants we store this energy in our bodies. We use the Sun's energy, which is produced by green life, essentially for nourishment and we use it to *fuel our blood, think,* see, hear, taste, smell and *feel.* In other words, *solar nuclear fusion ultimately furnishes the energy for most of our activities.*

Chapter VIII

Do you know why planet Earth is called "God's Green Earth"?

It is because every living form of green life serves an essential purpose in our overall well *Being*. Also, it is green life that *helps support life,* through the *production of oxygen.* We produce and exhale carbon dioxide, which is captured by God's Green Earth and then converted into oxygen in order to aide in our *conscious survival.*

Here's an interesting fact: coal, oil, and natural gas are all called fossil fuels, because they were formed from prehistoric plants and animals. And the chemical energy contained within these prehistoric plants and animals came from the *Sun.*

We use the chemical energy in fossil fuels to cook our food, warm our homes, run our cars, and make electricity. The energy from the Sun is *pure* and *clean.* We will not run out of solar energy any time soon. The Universal Sun will continue to provide us with solar energy for millions of years; thus the energy bestowed upon us from the Sun is *everlasting* and *renewable.*

<u>Now let's address the chemical composition of the human body</u>:

The adult human body averages 55–70% water. This percentage varies by age, sex, height, and weight. However, the water percentage, on average, within the human body contains 11% hydrogen by mass; but it also has a *hydrogen atomic abundance* of 67%. And these numbers, along with the corresponding percentage for oxygen in water, are the largest contributors to *overall mass and atomic composition* in the human anatomy.

Based on the water content in the human body, there is actually *more oxygen by mass* than any other element. However, there are more *hydrogen* atoms than any other element.

Now, what I am about to do is share the significance of each core element within the Sun, as it relates to their essential use to us human beings:

- Hydrogen* (essentially water)
- Helium (inert)
- Oxygen* (water/electron acceptor)
- Carbon (organic compounds)
- Iron* (hemoglobin)
- Sulfur (Cysteine, Methionine, Biotin, Thiamine)
- Nitrogen (DNA and Amino Acids)
- Magnesium (binds to ATP and other nucleotides)

So, what is the most common element required to maintain 'conscious life' on this planet? Well, you are correct if you said 'Oxygen'.

Also, what is the most abundant compound in the human body? You are correct if you said water. And finally, what is the chemical symbol for water? Correct H_2O; 2 parts Hydrogen and 1 part Oxygen.

Therefore it appears that the two most essential elements within the Sun—which are *Hydrogen* and *Oxygen*—are also the two primary elements within the human body, as well as, the two key components require for our Earthly existence.

Okay, now that I have concisely covered the scientific perspective of the composure of the Sun, along with our physical make up. Let's now reveal the *spiritual* connection that we all have with the Sun or *Center* of this Universe.

What I am about to do now is make my contribution to science!

What I am going to do is prove that there is no way that our human brain is physically equipped with a *conscious mind* or in other words, directly responsible for exuding our consciousness.

It is impossible for the human brain to be capable of producing the *intangible energy of consciousness;* considering the brain itself relies on the *energy of consciousness* in order to maintain 'ITS' own existence. Hence, our brain would not function without the essential energy of consciousness.

But first, allow me to ask you a few questions: Do you have an idea where consciousness could live? Do you believe there could be a logical explanation for where consciousness resides? Do you believe the mystery of life and consciousness can be less complex than what we 'subconsciously think'?

In other words, do you believe our 'man-made paradigms' make life more complicated than it is? And if so, then life should be indeed simple. Which in turn would mean there should be a simple explanation to define the hidden mystery to life, as well as, to the abstruse mystery surrounding the nature of consciousness?

Well, with all these questions in mind, please allow me to be the first soul to introduce you to the mystery of the human unknown:

Do you know what the scientific name is for consciousness?

Well guess what; it's **Oxygen!**

By mass, oxygen is the third-most abundant element in the universe, after hydrogen and helium. Many major classes of organic molecules in living organisms contain oxygen, such as proteins, nucleic acids, carbohydrates, and fats, as do the major constituent inorganic compounds of animal shells, teeth, and bone. Oxygen embodies most of the mass in living organisms, which is represented as a component of water, the major constituent of life-forms. Oxygen is also used in cellular respiration and is released by photosynthesis, which uses the *energy of sunlight* to produce oxygen from water and carbon dioxide.

Do you know that Living Cells are 'electromagnetic' units? In other words, do you realize that all cells are "lifeless" without electromagnetic energy?

By using the closed circuit systems when studying living cells, the scientists of today reject the obligatory existence of **magnetic fields** with **electric fields.**

Electricity and *magnetism* cannot be separated; hence they are aspects of the one phenomenon of *electromagnetism.* The fact changing electrical fields produce magnetic fields, and changing magnetic fields produce electrical fields has been forgotten by scientists that study living cells; therefore, the *electromagnetic* characteristics of all living cells in humans, animals, and plants—is misunderstood.

Mistaken theories in *biochemistry* have caused the wrong conclusions, especially as it relates to the nature of consciousness. Thus, believing that consciousness is a *biological substance* that is emitted directly from the brain is why this elusive phenomenon still remains a *"mystery."*

There are three molecular forms of Oxygen that comprise the Earth's Ozone layer and it is essentially this **conscious generating** element, which *absorbs* the 'electromagnetic' energy that is radiated by the Sun that we ultimately consume, that creates *living cells* within our physical body. Therefore, every cell within *any* physical form, including the *mysterious sinoatrial node,* is technically *dead* without the *life giving* element that we call oxygen. Hence, it is only through our absorption of oxygen, which contains *electromagnetic energy* that brings a dead cell to life; which theoretically says to me that the <u>universal nature of consciousness</u> is merely defined by **"electromagnetic energy."**

Einstein has shown us that the most long-standing theories may be open to drastic improvement. Therefore, the caveat is, we must be able to open and expand our minds to any plausible theory, even if our current state of mind makes it appear to be radical. Open criticism is the lifeblood of progress, as it relates to both science and cultures at large.

Chapter VIII

As mentioned above *oxygen* is the most *massive element* within the human body. And all other forms of life require oxygen for energy to also *maintain their conscious existence*. To be even more specific, all forms of life on this planet **sol**ely survives from one type of energy and that is ***solar energy***.

What scientists have deemed as oxygen is simply a scientific or technical term for *consciousness*.

<u>*Now, I ask you; how relevant is oxygen or consciousness to our overall well-being?*</u>

Well, before you begin to explore this question, please allow me to address it first, by providing you with a side-by-side example of how oxygen is actually a *synonym* for consciousness.

<u>*Did you know that out of all the natural elements needed by the human body, oxygen or consciousness is the primary one that we can't be minutes without?*</u>

Isn't it true that oxygen or *consciousness* is vital to our survival? Therefore, we human beings cannot *consciously live without oxygen* for more than a few minutes. Yet, this is an element most people don't even think could contribute to health problems. Although, nothing could be further from the truth.

You may not realize this, but one of the problems we are currently being faced with is oxygen or *consciousness* concentration levels in and around major cities has been measured, in some cases, to be 30% below normal. What this means is that each breath we take brings in less oxygen or less *consciousness,* which in essence *depletes our conscious awareness*. And as if this weren't bad enough, most people have developed poor breathing habits, thus further restricting oxygen or *consciousness* intake.

The resulting oxygen or *consciousness* deficiency is having a negative effect on our health, as well as, on our overall well-being.

Oxygen or *consciousness* deprivation can be associated with all kinds of chronic diseases, including cancer.

So let me ask you a vital question, when we pass out from not breathing, what is this commonly called? Is it called "un-oxygen"? Or is it called "unconscious"?

See, every single breath we take is indeed a *conscious breath of the solar energy of this Universe.* Thus, it is the *conscious energy of this Universe* that <u>grants 'conscious' life</u> to us all.

Now I am going to restate that we all share and are one with the same divine air we breathe. Every human being, regardless of the man-made concepts of *race, creed, origin, or religion* have one thing in common, and that is we all live and *consciously survive* from one *sacred supreme source of conscious electromagnetic energy,* which stems from this Universe.

So, with the above being outlined, please allow me to use the following as a prime example as to how we all share the same conscious energy, which is the only unseen 'soul' or 'spirit' of this Universe that conclusively defines every human being.

Okay, let's use mouth-to-mouth resuscitation as a prime example as how my and your physical existence is contingent upon the same sacred source of conscious energy. When there is a human being who is not breathing and is lying *unconscious* on the ground, and they are not at a terminal state, then mouth-to-mouth resuscitation can be used to restore *conscious life* back into this unconscious human shell.

<u>And do you know why mouth-to-mouth resuscitation was able to restore life back into this human form</u>?

Well, mouth-to-mouth resuscitation is able to *resurrect life* back into an unconscious human form through receiving the *universal* energy of consciousness from a conscious human being. Hence, the human shell is irrelevant without the divine conscious energy of this Universe.

<u>*Okay, allow me to further refine this example*</u>:

When a person is performing mouth-to-mouth resuscitation, the first thing they do is take a *BIG DEEP BREATH* which is essential to this process. Upon absorbing this big deep breath, this individual has now filled his lungs with universal consciousness. And once this individual consumes this sacred energy they will proceed to exhale the conscious electromagnetic energy from this Universe into the lungs of the unconscious human being.

Now, after *conscious energy* has been transferred into the lungs of the unconscious person, the individual who is performing mouth-to-mouth resuscitation will push down upon the chest of the unconscious body, which will in turn compress the *conscious filled lungs* of the unconscious human being.

Thus, the *'electro'-magnetic* energy from this Universe is then expelled from the unconscious individual's lungs, which then proceeds to *'spark'* the human heart, in order to regenerate and restore *conscious life* back into the unconscious human form.

So, let me ask you a question: Why do you think taking ten deep breaths is considered to be so beneficial?

Well for starters, taking ten deep breaths supplies us with *mental clarity*, increased energy, reduced muscle tension, and reduces physical stress. Though most importantly, taking ten deep conscious breaths provide us with *freedom from our subconscious mind*. Hence, conscious breathing seems to reconnect us to our universal nature.

Conscious breathing can become a wonderful tool, helping us to relax and reduce stress, improve our skin tone, sleep better, as well as losing inches and weight.

We have been breathing incorrectly for so long that we are not aware of how to properly breathe in order to receive maximum benefits from each breath we take. Once we establish how to effectively breathe we can then use each conscious breath as a stress destroyer. Many of us are unaware that we normally take shallow to minimal breathes; which in turn deprives us of our *conscious survival.*

Most people only use about twenty percent of their lung capacity. Frequent test have been performed, over-and-over-again to determine how much of our brain cells we actually use. Other tests have been done, in order to discover how our organs, such as our lungs, function. It is remarkable that we are all using a very *limited portion of our conscious potential* in all these areas.

It has been stated that approximately *seventy percent* of the *body's contaminants are eliminated from our bodies through breathing.* Why, because the solar energy that we breathe, from the *Sun,* is purifying. Therefore, when we accumulate toxins, due to ineffective breathing, we are actually inviting illness and disease to enter our bodies. Medical testing has proven again-and-again, that the missing link in those with cancer and other serious physical diseases is simply due to oxygen deprivation or in other words—*due to a lack of consciousness.*

On October 4, 2013 there was a study published in EMBO Molecular Medicine in which a noted Dartmouth researcher found that dying heart cells were kept alive with spikes of oxygen—or in other words *with spikes of consciousness.* Research revealed that during a heart attack, heart muscles actually start dying when the flow of oxygen-rich blood or *consciousness-rich blood* was interrupted as it attempted to migrate into specific sections of the heart.

When the human heart is deprived of oxygen or *consciousness* and other essential nutrients cell death occurs over a period of time leading to progressive loss of heart function and congestive heart failure.

Periannan Kuppusamy, PhD, Professor of Radiology at Geisel School of Medicine at Dartmouth, found that dying heart cells still contain enough oxygen or *consciousness* for metabolism, and additional short-term spikes of oxygen or *consciousness* kept the cells alive and active.

His research team used an animal model of acute myocardial infarction and discovered that daily administration of a higher concentration of oxygen or *consciousness,* for a short period of time each day, induced spikes in myocardial oxygenation, which prevented myocardial injury.

We all know that oxygen or *consciousness* is crucial for our survival, but it is also intriguing to know that the same oxygen or *consciousness* can be used like a drug to treat diseases.

*Please note I injected the word consciousness within the above written article.

See, what I have plugged into, is that there's nothing that defines me more than *Being* conscious, and I do mean nothing! And once we all tap into this profound sense of knowing, all our man-made beliefs that once made us snap will begin to detach themselves from our subconscious minds.

With all this mentioned, I am going to take this opportunity and revert back to a chapter where I stated that we are all the *Heirs of this Universe*. This means with every single breath we take, we are consuming the *conscious air of this Universe*. Hence, the air we all share is saturated with solar energy. And this conscious electromagnetic energy is a direct byproduct of the *Universal Sun*.

Thus, it is only through the Sun that we *"endure life";* hence without *consciousness* there is no life. And since we will never *physically* encounter the *conscious energy* of this Universe—*behold ITS only begotten Sun.*

So, with this being said, have you ever heard of the following expression: "You are what you eat?"

Well, don't you think the same rule should apply to, "You are what you breathe"?

Hence we are a unique unseen conscious energy which is defined by this Universe.

Just in case I may not have been crystal clear; the **sole** goal of this chapter is to make a sound attempt to shift our awareness towards the sacred truth, which is—only the Almighty conscious energy of this Universe, flows throughout our veins and provides us with the *spirit of life.* In further words, *it is not our physical form that creates conscious life, it is the consciousness of this Universe that brings every physical form to life.*

Therefore, we must understand that what we physically see is not me.

In other words, when we sense as sacred conscious Beings that our universal nature resides within all forms of life, then this is when this marvelous sense of knowing will make all forms of life *physically transparent.* This is when it will finally become *apparent* that you now *see me in you.* Only then will you come to know that **I AM** *everything* and *everything* is me.

Through this acknowledgment of truth, we will then be able to separate who we are from our man-made sense of self and then we will realize how independent we really are as divine conscious Beings. Hence, we will begin to know, that we no longer need to rely upon our man-made *self* in order to survive.

This means we will then come to know that we are not one with our ego and this discernment of truth will have finally set us free.

Chapter VIII

Thus, as it has been said, *"Only the truth can set you free," free from your subconscious mind.*

Now as it relates to I AM everything and everything is me, please allow me to be clear that this only applies to every form *of conscious life*. This means the *solar spirit of this Universe* that grants my human form life, is the exact same *solar energy* that bestows conscious life upon every other living form that resides on this glorious planet.

In other words, please take heed that, "I AM *everything* and *everything* is me" does not pertain to any existing man-made concept that governs my subconscious mind.

As I mentioned in a prior chapter, the following is the process I was referring to as it relates to eliminating our 'self' in order for 'us' to be born again.

Now, in order for our man-made *self* to die, *we* must first acknowledge what authentically defines us. And once we become aware that we are the *awareness,* or in other words, once we become deeply conscious of the fact that we are indeed the *consciousness of this Universe;* then this level of knowing will be the catalyst towards extinguishing our *self.*

Once your subconscious mind has been *enlightened* with the awareness of the *true you,* this degree of insight will then fade away the *man-made self-image,* of who you think you are.

So, once we have divorced our *self* and *we* and *our awareness* have been reunited, then we can proceed to inform our subconscious mind of this enlightening union. Now at this point of awareness our ego has no choice but to hand over our precious life and set the soul of who we are free. Thus, the beauty in discovering that we are Conscious Beings of this Universe, allows us to gain more conscious control of our life. Considering, there is nothing outside of the nature of consciousness that truly defines us.

God's Immortal Soul (Sol)

See, the main reason we have formed a lasting relationship with our ego is because we have not recognized that we are indeed the *divine conscious observer* within our human form.. It is only through the *'Wholly' spirit that resides within the Sun* which circulates throughout our divine air that bestows upon our human forms the *mysterious nature of consciousness.*

<u>Even with all this said, you may be still wondering how in the world do we actually go about gaining our conscious independence</u>.

<u>Well here's how</u>:

There is only one reason we think that we are one with our ego. This is because we are under the notion that our *man-made beliefs* are what define us.

See, we undoubtedly believe that our *physical image, origin, culture, religion, profession, political affiliation, etc.,* are all the things that define who we are. And since we profoundly believe that these man-made concepts define us, our paradigms are able to manipulate us.

Thus, once our paradigms consume our attention, our ego becomes equipped to exploit our awareness and control our lives. As sacred conscious Beings of this Universe, the only way we will ever gain our conscious independence is through knowing that *only love* defines us. And outside of this **sacred emotion** there is absolutely *no man-made concept* that is stored within our subconscious mind that represents who we are.

And I do mean—*absolutely nothing!*

See, before any man-made concept is captured by our subconscious mind love is the first notion of an emotion that is instilled within our human heart during our inaugural *conception.*

Therefore, not even our innate talents define who we are considering these special talents that we are blessed with only determine our unique natural or physical capabilities. And despite what we

Chapter VIII

may believe, not even the Cities, States, Islands, or Countries that we are born into, which we proclaim to be our own encompasses our true identity. There is no human being who is entitled to any Country or any land.

And not even our names, which people tend to inquire about in order to get a man-made sense for who we are, represent our identities. The same is true for our nationalities such as: Italian; Spanish; German; etc. Thus, our last names which are often a reflection of our nationalities, are simply labels that are used to identify the man-made image of who we think we are.

And, as it pertains to our designated countries, which we go to war for, please know that no human being was born or destined to defend and die for any '*man-made*' government or for any region for any reason. In reality, no part of Mother Earth belongs to us, we belong to her; thus our reason for *Being* is to *lovingly* share her and not to go war over her.

Okay now, please allow me this moment to shed some light as to why not even our cultures define who we are. And how our cultures, regardless of how much we love and are attached to them, are in reality nothing more than our **initial** *conscious experience.*

So with this being stated, please allow me to restate that as conscious beings, we must try to understand that *love* is the only true substance that defines us as *divine* human beings and nothing else.

<u>*Therefore, as it relates to believing that our cultures define us, how about trying to perceive it from this angle*</u>:

Let's say that you are in the military and you happen to get deployed to one of the following Countries: Iraq, Japan, or Afghanistan for over a year. So tell me, does this year long deployment within these other cultures now mean that you are Iraqi, Japanese, or Afghani? Chances are no! Considering, in most cases you will simply chalk this up as a *life or conscious experience* and nothing more.

Well, the same rule applies to the cultures that we are born into. See, the individual cultures that we are born into and are raised in merely define our *initial and overall conscious experience in life* and nothing more.

Each culture that we are born into becomes our *primary conscious experience*. And since we have no real idea who we really are, we are conditioned to believe that our cultures define who we are.

Now, despite this cultural misconception, our mission while we are here on this sacred planet is not to believe that certain man-made concepts define us. Hence, these man-made encounters should only be stored within our subconscious mind; in order to *simply define our conscious experience.*

In other words all the information compiled within our subconscious library determines as a conscious Being what we have *consciously encountered physically,* what we have *consciously experienced conceptually,* and what *ideas and lessons we have consciously learned along the way.*

Therefore, we need to awaken to the fact that every man-made concept and idea that we have consciously encountered while being here does not define us. It only defines what we have consciously experienced during our Earthly exploration and that is it!

Quite frankly I have nothing against the premise of our cultural concepts. I honestly feel that it is fascinating how we human beings have created unique and interesting ways to consciously experience life, hence, once again, the key word being *experience.*

So, please try to realize, everything we confront within this realm of reality is nothing more than a *conscious encounter* or a *conscious experience.* And what genuinely serves us goes far beyond the *birth* of any *man-made concept that has matured within our subconscious minds.* And although, our individual cultures are responsible for having an impact on our personal behaviors, no one's cultural behavior should be guilty of altering their universal loving nature.

Maybe when we recognize that our cultures only define our *deep-rooted conscious experience* while residing here on Earth, we would be more apt to share, as well as be open to another soul's cultural experience versus believing that it is not in our nature to know another man's culture.

As human beings, our reason for *Being* is to share and embrace another human *Being's life or conscious experience.* And once we awaken to the fact that our subconscious mind is a warehouse for what we have consciously encountered, then we will be able to separate who we are from our limiting beliefs which will in turn grant us our *"conscious independence."*

Hence, once we obtain our conscious independence we will begin to grasp that our subconscious mind is a sacred tool, which we as conscious Beings have been blessed with in order to assist and aide us during our conscious journey while residing here on this glorious planet. In other words we will then comprehend that our subconscious mind is indeed our *soul's mate.*

Please discern the only reason our subconscious mind currently owns us is because we *completely depend on it to define us.* Thus, every deceptive man-made concept that we give our life or our attention to tends to devour our divinity.

Therefore, what we must come to acknowledge is the following: *My subconscious mind will never be divine until it is mine!* Once we introduce our divine nature to our subconscious mind, our subconscious mind will then proceed to cultivate itself with a more glorious landscape.

So in summary, without the conscious energy of this Universe the human shell is hollow. And if we never discover that it is only the conscious energy of this Universe that defines us then we will always bear a *shallow perception* of who we think we are.

Therefore, the next time you are outside, please do your *'self'* a favor and tilt your head back and inhale a big deep breath of *universal consciousness.*

Now with all this being said, please allow me to reiterate that the divine conscious energy of this Universe, which we absorb, is received through the Sun. Hence, this *shining* reflection of this Universe, is what represents the *soul* of every conscious Being, on this conscious planet.

In other words, *we are all one with the Universal Sun,* considering we all consume its divinity through the sacred air we breathe. And through the divine air we breathe we are all united as children of this Universe or, in other words, *Heirs* of the same loving family.

<u>*Even with all this, some may be inclined to inquire; well if the Sun of this Universe is considered to be so beneficial to our overall well-being, then why does it possess the potential to be so harmful to us*</u>?

Well, the only logical response to this question would be if our diets did not consist of processed foods and we were more in harmony with the natural harvest that Mother Earth provides via the Sun's love, then the Sun's radiance may not be so harmful to us.

In other words, if we feasted directly from Mother Earth, Father Sun would probably be more nurturing. Also, if we human beings weren't so *self-destructive* by destroying the ozone layer, through releasing poisonous toxins in the divine air that we breathe we would most likely be able to rid ourselves of numerous ailments and diseases.

Well speaking of ailments and diseases, do you realize this Universe is not responsible for the diseases that plague humanity?

Chapter VIII

Mother Earth was born *clean and pure*, by way of Father Sun, and it is only the ill nature of man that has given birth to diseases that plague this world; from cancer to AIDS.

In other words, it is the man-made nature of humanity that is the disease which infects this Universe and affects the balance of all nature.

So, based upon the above information, do you still believe that our consciousness stems or originates from our human brain? Or do you now sense that the sacred energy of consciousness bears its own independence?

Do you sense that every aspect of our existence is surrounded by solar energy?

Do you now detect that our conscious existence is a direct byproduct of being showered by the conscious electromagnetic energy that radiates from the Sun?

And finally I have a random question for you. Do you believe that our planet is an equal member of the Solar System?

Well, if you answered yes to the final inquiry—then guess what? *El Sol* is our **Solar System**. Without the Sun, there would be no planet Earth.

Remember, the Sun constitutes approximately 99.86% of the mass of our Solar System. This makes it the *enlightening nucleus* or the beacon of *Wholly* Enlightenment within our Universe and from my perspective we human beings are a reflection of our *Solar System*.

It is presumed that our Solar System was formed from a gravitational *singularity* and our human system is formed from a *single* zygote cell. And *El Sol* is the nucleus, which maintains the existence of *conscious life* within our *physical planet* and our *soul/sol* is the nucleus that maintains *conscious life* within our *physical form.* Thus, our physical *system* is created to contain the *solar energy* of who we are.

According to scientists, Father Sun is who gave birth to Mother Earth. And speaking of Father Sun, in my opinion, it is actually Father Sun that represents the Christian Trinity.

The pure *Wholly* spirit or *'light'* from Father Sun is the *Father,* the *Sun,* and the *Holy 'Wholly' spirit of enlightenment.* Hence, this represents the only *rational* explanation as to how *Father God, His Sun, and the Holy Spirit* are all one in the same.

It is truly breathtaking to know that the *sacred conscious spirit of this Universe* is bestowed upon us through every single breath we take.

So, in 'light' of all the above information, let's proceed to unveil the real 'Sun of God'.

God's Sun is the risen or *resurrected* Savior, which rises every morning. *God Sun* is the light that shines its radiance upon this world. *God Sun* is the light that shines bright within all of humanity. *God Sun* is what can be seen in the Heavens.

Hence, *God Sun is the only begotten Sun of this Universe.*

In reality, religion was born from spirituality and spirituality is based upon the conscious loving energy of this Universe that is poured down upon us by way of the Sun.

In my opinion, the primary controversy that discredits the Christian religion is that the life story of Jesus seems to mirror other previous *mythical* Gods with similar attributes. The Biblical story of Jesus appears to be another representation of other ancient mythical Gods that were represented as God's true Sun by man him *'self'*.

In other words, *the Jesus life story is an illustration of a modern day 'Solar' Deity or* **"Sun God."** In reality, the life story of Jesus outlined throughout the Bible is merely a depiction of the Sun's migration throughout a calendar year.

<u>Here's what I mean:</u>

The resurrection and the supposed birth of Jesus Christ is presumed to be on December 25, 1 AD. During this time of year something fascinating appears to take place. The Sun of God, on December 22, which is usually the beginning of the winter solstice, seems to pause or *die* for *three days* on a southern constellation also referred to as the Southern Crux or the *Southern Cross.*

Now, just after the Sun of God is seemingly resurrected and born again on December 25, God's Sun begins to make its way back towards the Northern Hemisphere and *miraculously* begins to *restore life* back into the dead winter crops, plants, and trees. Although the Sun's resurrection seems to take place during the latter part of December, it is actually celebrated during the spring equinox which is *Easter.*

God's Sun will ultimately reach its highest point in the sky to supposedly sit next to throne of his Heavenly Father, during the latter part of June which is called the summer solstice.

See, this is why **Sunday** is considered to be the sacred day of worship, because there is nothing that is more sacred than the **Sun.** Hence, *it is **solely** the Universal Sun that is the Creator of all universal life.*

However, as I stated earlier, I do believe that there was a highly enlighten human being that once walk this earth amongst us. And although there is no physical evidence of Jesus' existence, for me it is through the way the Jesus scripture speaks to me that helps support my belief in him. I am sure this is apparent based upon the numerous Jesus scriptures that are outlined throughout this book. Thus, I sense the loving scripture of Jesus is indeed a concept, or an example, that we should all live by.

Nevertheless, feeling that the Jesus scripture is bona fide does not make me believe that the embellished Bible story of Jesus is also true.

Therefore with this being said, please allow me to ask you a few 'religious' questions.

Why do you think humanity believes in religion?

Do you think we 'fear not' believing in religion, more so than we actually believe in religion? Do you think it's because we must believe in something? Do you think we human beings are hopeless; therefore religion provides us with some form of aspiration? Do you think it's a herd mentality whereas we only believe in some form of religion, simply because everyone else appears to? Or do you think it's primarily because we have spent our entire lives believing in some form of religion and based upon this significant down payment of giving our lives to our elected religion(s), we are ultimately expecting a 'Heavenly' return?

Now, if the religion you have chosen to worship provides you with a sense of community and a feeling of commonality and you are someone who makes a grand effort towards living your life according to the Jesus scripture, than kudos to you.

However, if you are someone who worships your religion thinking that it will be the platform that will someday catapult you into a more Heavenly reality—well needless to say, you are someone who is not sincerely working towards being a more loving or giving human being.

It is because you are more focused on what your *selfishness* will bring? In other words, are you *selfishly* expecting a Heavenly return on your invested belief, by way of partially believing in your religion, in order to *"save your**self**"*?

Chapter VIII

Although, as it really relates to our religious convictions, if we are completely honest with our*selves*, we would admit that we only tithe and relinquish our lives to our chosen religion(s) for one reason and one reason only; and that is to *selfishly* gain something in return.

Please correct me if I am wrong, but no one worships their religious God who is not expecting some sort of *Heavenly* transcendence.

It also appears that we human beings are under the impression that our Religious Temples are established to provide us with *spiritual nourishment;* when in reality these Religious Temples are only built to supply their congregation with *religious reinforcement.*

What I find fascinating about religion, especially as it relates to the Christian religion, is the moment their God is compared to the *nature of the Sun,* Christian leaders tend to get anxious and start screaming that this is blaspheme and proclaim that this is the Devil talking and He's trying to steer you away from the truth.

And then they proceed to quote **Matthew 7:15** which proclaims you need to *"beware of false prophets!"* And the only reason these Christian leaders want us to beware of so called false prophets is because if we don't, then they will no longer *profit* from our religious beliefs. Well, if you ask me, we all need to *beware of false propaganda.*

See, one of the key distinctions between Spirituality and Religion, is Spirituality tends to be uplifting and is centered around the *true nature of this Universe living within all forms of life,* whereas most religions focus on filling our subconscious mind with man-made *lies* which steal our divine nature right before our eyes, by making us *'believe'* that the divinity of this Universe *'lies'* only within one *'male'* image.

Religion also acts as a form of business; which means most religions are in the business of making human beings believe in *debatable Gods*. Religion uses biblical scriptures such as *"beware of false prophets"* as a form of reverse psychology in order to defend their *unfounded* God(s).

In other words, religion is a *multi-billion* dollar business which solely cashes in on our beliefs. The real energy of this Universe does not live in religion. *The conscious spirit of this Universe only resides in the presence of reality.*

This means the *conscious spirit of this Universe* is the source of life that naturally manifests our *conscious reality*, hence the word *Spirituality* or *Spiritual "Reality"*. And in truth Jesus was not a Religious Preacher, He was a *Spiritual Teacher*. Therefore, if you ask me, Jesus really wouldn't appreciate being worshipped in such a *"Religious"* manner. Considering, it has been stated that Jesus once said:

"Religion makes man ignorant to the truth!"

See, the only reason we believe that this Universe is in the form of man, is because the Bible says we are all made in God's image. And considering we think our *physical image* is what define us we subconsciously perceive this Universe as being this man-made entity.

Therefore, the *man-made image of this Universe* that we have been conditioned to believe and worship is nothing more than a figment of our man-made imagination. The divine nature of this Universe is not defined by anything that is physical or material. This Universe represents the spiritual sacred energy of love. Hence, *it is indeed the divine nature of love that we are all made of.*

The real reason Christian leaders do not want us to direct our attention towards the *true nature of this Universe* and exclusively as it relates to the Universe's *"True Sun"* is because they know if we begin to grant our awareness towards this *nature of knowing*, it will expose the *grandest man-made lie* ever told to humanity.

Chapter VIII

Beyond what we have been conditioned to believe, *more truth lays within the Sun, than within our Religious beliefs.*

Please, at your leisure, the next time you view a Jesus painting or a photograph of Jesus. I invite you to pay close attention to what other image is shown within the painting or within the photograph that is representing Jesus. Chances are you will notice that the *Sun* is either behind the head of Jesus or Jesus himself will be shown raising his palms to the sky, basking in the glory of the Sun.

See, what we have been conditioned to believe as being a *halo* surrounding Jesus' head, is really nothing more than an illusion. Jesus' head is actually placed within the *center of the Sun;* which projects the illusion of what man calls a halo. So, please know it is the Sun, which we have been conditioned to shun that we obtain true enlightenment from.

What I find fascinating is that it has been 2000 years, and due to our man-made beliefs we have yet to comprehend Jesus' divine message or his true mission for us to pursue *Wholeness.* Considering our attention is so fixated on man's story of the messenger we have failed to *interpret the messenger's real message.*

In my opinion; Jesus was a messenger of the *light;* which is why He was considered to be an *en-'light'-ened* messenger. Hence, the real premise of Jesus' Holy *Wholly* mission was to try to have humanity envision that the *'Sun' of God* is also the *'Sun' of Man.*

Or in other words, *the Sun of this Universe is actually the conscious solar energy that lives and shines within Man or within all humanity.* Thus, only through this degree of en**light**enment will our divine light shine and make us all the *light of this world.*

<u>Which leads me to the following question, what does enlightenment mean to you?</u>

Well to me enlightenment means *consciously plugging into the reality* that we are indeed the *solar light of this Universe* that shines within our human form.

Now let me ask you, do you ever wonder why a sunset makes us feel so peaceful inside?

<u>Well, maybe the following can 'shine some light' on why we all feel a certain way upon saying good night to the glorious Sun of God.</u>

I know it's difficult to bear witness to the love that shines our way; considering we cannot stare upon its glory in any way.

It's not until Father Sun bids farewell to another day, does God's Sun say; now my children you may look my way.

As we behold the beauty of the Sun of God saying goodnight; it's one of the most tranquil moments to witness through sight.

God's setting Sun shares an affectionate emotion which is 'soul/sol' for real. God's Sun provides us with an essence of how love should really feel.

Through God's Sol; we embrace a loving tie to that miraculous symbol in our sky.

As we glance at the symmetry of enlightening romance; our spirit begins to dance.

And upon our Father's daily adieu, we can sense a silent whisper that says; goodnight my children, I love you!

Now based upon this enlightening or *'in-lightening'* poem; if you are someone who still has doubts in regards to our relationship with the Sun, I ask you one very simple question:

*When the Sun is shining bright; does it **naturally** 'fill/feel' you with de**light**?*

Chapter VIII

Question: Do you believe, based upon the 'selfish love' that we have formed for so many different versions of God, that we can all COEXIST?

See, the reason I ask this question is because I usually notice the expression "COEXIST" stuck on the back bumper of automobiles. And although this is a nice gesture, I feel *unity* is unattainable for those who believe *passionately* that their religion is the one and only religion that accurately defines this Universe. Therefore, based upon a distinct difference in religious beliefs, this alone makes the summons to *coexist* a monumental request.

See, the only way humanity will ever be able to *coexist* is through knowing that only *one God exists,* and this *sole God* is what lives within every human being. And through the acknowledgement of a *solo God,* one discovers *one love*. And by way of one love, unity is formed. And through unity we all encounter Heaven.

In other words, in order for humankind to *coexist* and experience Heaven on Earth; *this man-made notion that there are different male deities that represent this Universe must no longer exist.*

Okay, speaking of 'coexist'; Religion and Science to this day, still have their differences of opinion as it relates to an unseen Universal energy that we human beings refer to as God.

Christianity believes that life is a form of divine creation and Science believes that life is a form of evolution.

Well, allow me ask you a question: Do you believe a ceremony could be performed, between Christianity and Science, whereas we would be willing to say 'I DO' to both Christianity and Science?

<u>Well, here's how I have married Christianity and Creation with Science and Evolution.</u>

Christianity and Creation:

Well 'I DO' agree that life is an intangible miracle that is created by this divine Universe. However, I do not feel that life itself is a *form* of evolution. Considering, *there is nothing physical about life*; which means in theory, life can't evolve. Since, life is static, life is unchangeable and life is everlasting.

Life is actually the *sacred energy* that is *created* to animate our physical form, which means there is no such thing as *"physical energy."*

Science and Evolution:

Well 'I DO' agree that the human form, *which contains life*, has evolved.

The human form, as it is compared to other physical forms of life on this planet, is the most *evolved* and *sophisticated* organism ever designed. And it is the human brain, or subconscious mind if you will, that exemplifies the *sophisticated evolution* of the human structure. Hence, the human brain is what makes us human beings an advanced or *evolved physical form* of sacred life.

Oh, and let's not forget to address the argument that some scientists have in regards to the Christian concept of a *living soul*.

Well, believe it or not—Science and Christianity, <u>minus the Christian God concept</u> can *coexist*.

See, whether science realizes this or not, via their exploration of the Sun they have inadvertently proven that we are all *living souls/sols,* considering our lives are all contingent upon the *Solar energy from the Sun;* which brings me to the following passage:

As we all know the majority of the verbiage written within the Holy Bible is strictly up for personal interpretation. However, for those of us who are followers of the Christian faith, one is taught to believe that every written word in the Bible is

Chapter VIII

unquestionably God's word, so therefore every word should be obeyed.

Although, do you know what I find astonishing? Even amidst all the cloudy scripture that is communicated throughout the Bible, there is one proclamation in the Bible that stands out and is crystal clear in terms of its meaning, as it pertains to what defines us. And yet, even in 'light' of this direct reference to who we are, some of us still misconstrue the obvious. And this profound declaration precisely states that we are all 'living souls'!

So, in light of this proclamation, why do you think Christians are *disobedient* in regards to this direct reference toward us being living souls? Meaning, why do you think Christians, in light of this clear cut scripture elect to believe that we *have* a soul versus knowing that **we are the soul**? Or better yet, why do you think those of us who are Christians, are not as passionate about believing that we are living souls, as much as we are adamant about believing that God is a perfect and powerful man who rules this Universe?

Well, believe it or not, the answer is quite simple. The main reason we do not embrace being living souls is because the idea that we are living souls has not been <u>'religiously drilled'</u> into our psyche.

See, if we could find the courage to look beyond the premise surrounding our religious beliefs we would notice that man *insistently* preaches that this Universe is in the image of only *one* Supreme Being and never in turn preaches to the contrary.

In other words, man only works to *religiously reinforce* the concept that this Universe lives only in the form of *one* Omnipotent Man that we should all fear and worship versus introducing us to the truth, which is that the *divine soul of this Universe* rests and resides in the form of every human being.

And do you know why Religion chooses not to place much emphasis on the Biblical notion that we are all living souls?

Well, if religion were to frequently remind us human beings that we all share and are one with the same divine 'Sol' of this Universe which makes us all living souls, and that we are all interconnected and interwoven by the universal energy of love, then what would happen to religion?

Religion would *perish* and we human beings would *flourish*!

See, in truth Man's Religion distorts our perception and deceives us, in order to maintain its own survival.

I know some of us may not see the *monumental* difference that rest between believing that we *have* a soul versus *knowing* that we are the soul, as if to say: what is the big difference? However, the irony is this *misperception* in itself is what makes all the *difference in the world!*

Thus I ask, if **you** proclaim *that you* have a soul, yet do not declare that you are the soul, which is *the conscious observer, the thinker, the energy, the life, the light, and the love* that shines bright within **your** human form; then what do you think defines the real essence, or energy, of **you**?

Now, if one has decided to explore this question by way of fumbling through the man-made concepts that clutter their sub-conscious mind I can assure you with great certainty that they will not discover a solid answer that will accurately define who they are.

And do you know why?

Well, because if we choose to believe that we have a soul versus knowing that we are a *living soul,* then do you know what this grave *misconception* translates to us being?

A living man-made concept!

Chapter VIII

Now, based upon this information this is where we as human beings must be willing to say 'I DO' to both Christianity and Science.

We human beings must 'Will' our 'selves' to evolve as a sophisticated form of life in order to realize that *we are all a creation of divine energy* that is *formed* by a divine unseen Universal source of immeasurable power.

So, with all this said, please allow me to solidify this 'Wholly' matrimony between Christianity and Science by finally providing you with my perception as to why we human beings are considered to be 'living souls':

As I mentioned earlier in this chapter, all living Beings are represented by an *immortal soul.* And the synonyms I displayed earlier to define the sacred soul were as follows: *consciousness, life, Being, energy, spirit, the* **light,** and last but not least, the power of love.

Now, here's my intuitive definition of a *bodiless soul*: All living Beings contain and share the energy of the Sun or in other words the **Sol** of this Universe. And although we spell the human soul as *soul*; I am going to temporarily rename the word soul and spell it as *sol*; because from my perspective it is only the **sol**e electromagnetic energy of *El Sol* that fuels every aspect of our *Being*.

In other words; our human forms are *lifeless* without the *conscious inclusion of the Sun/Sol of this Universe.* Hence, I am a Living *'Soul/Sol'*.

And did you know that the Sun is one massive Atom? And with this being asked, based upon scientific evidence, hasn't it been proven that every human being is made of Atoms?

Well, as living *'souls/sols'*, we are comprised of Hydrogen; which is *the most common 'Atomic' element within the Sun, as well as, within the human body.* And we are also saturated with

Oxygen or as I prefer to say *consciousness;* which is *the largest element by mass within the human body.* Therefore, as *children of the Sun*; we are all unique *Atomic Structures of Universal Consciousness.*

Thus, beyond what we see we are all the truth, the life, the 'light' and the way.

However, let me replace the "u" back into the word *sol*; because the truth that lies beyond our man-made belief is; *'you'* are indeed the immortal *'soul/sol'* of this Universe!

See, once we awaken to the fact that it is the conscious energy from the Universe's *immortal Sun/Sol* that defines us and not our *mortal form,* we will then cease judging another human being by his or her human cover. And we will then be able to see beyond our man-made facades and acknowledge that we are all *uniquely the same.*

We are all *unique* divine Beings that are one with the *same* conscious energy that stems from *'one'* Sun. This marvelous understanding will cure our myopia and allow us to envision that we are all stitched together by the same universal thread; *which is love.*

And once we recognize that we are all linked to the same loving family; this degree of knowing will then manifest into *one love,* which also translates into **Soulove.**

Therefore, awakening to our true divine nature will aide us to realize; that in *spiritual* essence we are:

Solar Beings living life as

One adjoined to only *one* Sun

United *Solely* through its

L OVE

Chapter VIII

So, for a true peace of subconscious mind, let's all *lighten* up and let the love that defines us shine. Thus, again as Jesus said, *"We are all the light of this world!"*

Therefore, we must all discern that only through the construction of unity will we ever create harmony. And harmony is the only true recipe for genuine peace, love, and happiness.

With all this being uncovered, some individuals may still proclaim that I speak in a Native tongue, and some may even say that I speak of a Pagan religion. Well regardless of what one prefers to call it, please don't forget to call what it is, *The 'Whole' Truth!*

The Christian religion speaks of the truth in terms of love, consciousness, and forgiveness; unfortunately, these truths stand upon a *lying* platform which has been constructed by a manmade belief that embrace an extremely irrational story about who represents this Universe, without any real moral support. Hence, it makes this shaky belief that sits upon this unstable religious platform that is <u>preached by man</u> very unreliable.

This *man-made belief* that we have in terms of our religious God(s) is nothing more than a man-made concept that has been drilled into our subconscious psyche since childhood. And this is when religion tends to capitalize on our subconscious exposure and then *preys* upon us, so that we can spend a lifetime *praying* upon it. This is why religion says, *hand over your children at the age of five and they will become believers for life.*

Although we are taught as young naive children to believe in some form of religion, it will only be through the maturity of discovering who we really are that will allow us to outgrow these childish beliefs. And via the discovery of our true nature, we will then acknowledge that the only reason churches stay filled, is because every *lost soul* that enters into these Religious Chapels are still *seeking true fulfillment*.

However, once you plug into the true you, this level of enlightenment will *illuminate* your subconscious mind; which will in turn shine the light upon your religious belief and expose it for what it is. This true sense of knowing will then begin to leave each religious temple *lying empty*, and our subconscious mind will have finally become *filled with the whole truth.*

See, we currently rely on religion, because we have nothing else to rely on, and we surely can't depend on our***selves.***

However, if we were to coherently tap into our true nature, which is love, then we would not feel the need to top it off with accepting so many different and unverifiable versions of this Universe as being our true Redeemer.

See, once we awaken to our true nature, *this will encourage us to exude genuine love towards other human beings,* and this gesture alone will then trump the desire to worship any *irrational man-made notion of this Universe.*

Okay, now that I have shared my theory, I ask you this essential question. As living souls/sols, what is our sole purpose for being here?

<u>Well, here is a list for starters</u>:

- Our **sol**e (soul) purpose for being here is to be filled with joy.

- Our **sol**e (soul) purpose for being here is to create peace and harmony.

- Our **sol**e (soul) purpose for being here is to respect all forms of life.

- Our **sol**e (soul) purpose for being here is to appreciate and love Mother Earth and Father Sun.

- And last but not least; our **sol**e (soul) purpose for being here is to love and be loved!

Chapter VIII

Following you will find Biblical scriptures that represent the Sun of God.

"All things came into being by [Christ/*Sun*], and apart from Him nothing came into being that has come into being. In Him was life; and the *life was the light* of men" (John 1:3, KJV).

Translation: *All conscious life comes into being through God's Sun; hence the Sun is the "Sun of God", as well as, the "Sun of Man."*

"I am the *light of the world;* he who follows me shall not walk in the darkness, but shall have the *light of life*" (John 8:12, KJV).

"In Jesus *(The Sun of God)* was life, and the life was the *light of men*" (John 1:4, KJV).

Jesus told his disciples, "You are the *light of the world*" (Matthew 5:14, KJV).

Translation: *The Sun of God is the 'light of life' that shines within every living Being.*

"I am the way, and the truth, and the life; no one comes to the Father, but through me" (John 14:6, KJV).

Translation: *God's Sun is the way, the truth and the life. Hence; God's Sun is the closest we will ever get to witness the Creator or the Father that resides beyond the Sun.*

"I am with you always, even to the end of the Age" (Matthew 28:20, KJV). *His followers ask who to look to next. He tells them to follow the man with* **the bucket of water (Enki) and go into his house. Enki of the Anunnaki is that man with the bucket of water.**

Translation: *As of 1 AD which is the presumed birth of Christ. The Sun entered into the Age of Pisces, the fish, (which is a symbol that is used to represent Jesus). Now, as we approach 2150 AD, it*

God's Immortal Soul (Sol)

is presumed that we will be entering into the Age of Aquarius the sign that represents the water bearer. Of course the reference to an 'Age' and the time frame that is associated with an Age vary based upon man's personal opinion.

However, in 2150 AD the Sun, in accordance with the precession of the equinoxes, will then migrate into a New Age called; "The Age of Aquarius."

<u>Please allow me to expand upon the Age of an equinox</u>:

The precession of the equinoxes or the precession of the *spring equinox* is a motion of the equinoxes along the ecliptic plane of Earth's orbit caused by the cyclic precession of Earth's axis of rotation. During this process, the twelve astrological signs instead of progressing forward, as they would throughout a calendar year, precede backwards.

The precession age is approximately 2,150 years and the precession of the spring equinoxes began in 4300 BC with the astrological sign of *Taurus the Bull*. And then preceded with *Aries the Ram*; hence the *Biblical Story* surrounding Moses blowing the rams horn in 2150 B.C. And then in 1 AD, this is when the Sun entered into the age of *Pisces the Fish*; thus, this is when the Biblical life story of Jesus was born.

However, it is vital that we human beings *awaken* to our divine nature and comprehend the true meaning of Jesus' sacred mission before the *Christian God concept of Jesus* comes to an end. Considering, once we enter into the Age of Aquarius; who will we *worship then?*

I sense that the *soul, spirit, or life* of Jesus has moved on; therefore don't you think we should do the same?

Thus, once our conscious experience is over within this Earthly realm of reality our soulful spirit will also move on and to where no one knows. Hence, the expression; *"life moves on."* And let's face it, there will always be certain profound things that we may never be privy to and where our *solar energy* will reside after this realm of reality is indeed one of those esoteric unknowns.

Therefore, for any human being to believe in man's concept of *Heaven or Hell*, which of course has yet to be detected or disclosed, is nothing more than another way man's religion is able to rule us through the powerful *subconscious emotion* we call *fear*.

Even with this being said I fathom why certain human beings still have faith that Jesus will one day return, despite the fact that it has been supposedly two millenniums.

What's intriguing is our belief in Jesus' return is completely contingent upon our prayers. Whenever we pray to Jesus or to any other religious version of this Universe *specifically by name*, and if our prayers are answered this seemingly miraculous response to our prayers provides us with reassurance that our elected God(s) may truly exist.

Hence, as a Christian believer this restores our faith that there is still a strong possibility that Jesus may someday return.

Please note I will expand upon why this belief is nothing more than a subconscious illusion in an upcoming chapter.

In the world of *genuine reality* there is nothing that is more sacred than the Sun. Although, what I find astonishing is we human beings are so lost within the darkness of our paradigms that we can't even sense the *truth that shines brightly* upon us each and every day. And as it relates to having *faith* and *hope* in the '*Sun' of God,* well the Sun's radiance grants us with *hope every day* that there will always be a *brighter tomorrow.*

Now, here are my final words related to Christianity or any other religion for that matter:

God's Immortal Soul (Sol)

If any religion makes you love and worship only their idea of this Universe over anything else, then your religion is doing you a serious injustice.

Once we encounter the pleasure of experiencing the Universe's true nature, we will then know that this Universe does not require or desire to be worshipped. All this Universe wants for us is to find peace, joy, and harmony in order to form a more loving planet.

However, if we examine our religious beliefs, we will realize how *self-centered* and *egotistical* most religious Gods are. In other words, the man-made Gods that we have been groomed to *religiously worship* are more *selfish* than *selfless*. Considering, they command and demand so much from us.

In reality we are '*solely/souly*' putting forth all the *emotional* leg work in order to determine if our prayers will be answered. Yet, our religious Gods receive all the glory. Hence, our religions are not really trying to accomplish world *peace* because their *man-made mission* seems to be more centered on trying to achieve a Universal piece of us.

See, whether we accept this or not, it is only our religious beliefs that breed Terrorists—considering we are intensely terrified of our religious Gods. And this acute sense of terror is what drives our*selves* to do terribly *selfish* and senseless things to our fellow human beings. In other words; *we do not naturally love to embrace our religious Gods, as much as we **fear** letting them go.*

Please correct me if I am wrong but I often hear people profess that "I am a God *fearing* Man." However to the contrary, I never hear anyone confess that they are a *"God loving Man."* I sincerely hope that you find this information *alarming, because it is meant* to serve as a *wakeup call.*

Therefore *rise and shine* and let's be the *shining stars* that we were meant to be.

IX

Our Heart's Sole (Sol) Purpose

Did you know the human heart is more than just a 10 oz. organ?

Did you know the human heart can beat outside the body and it powers our life giving 'electromagnetic' blood through 60,000 miles of our circulatory system, which is nearly 2.5 times around the Earth?

Did you know that every conscious life form on earth has a heart?

<u>How is the human heart connected to the Universe</u>?

New information about the human heart indicates that it could be the very first connection point between the human body and the Universe. The heart begins to beat in the unborn fetus even before the brain is formed. So, it appears that the heart is an early '<u>sustainer</u>' of human life.

Inside the human body there is a perpetual blizzard of information processing, message passing, electrochemical processes, hormones, enzymes, and physical activity. Central to all this 24/7 activity is the brain which is always active, even during sleep. The heart, another vital and constantly active organ, is in constant contact with the brain via nerve action potentials and hormonal pathways. Independently the brain and the heart generate dynamic *electromagnetic fields* as a byproduct of their nervous activities.

In addition, the heart muscle contractions produce fields of their own. All these fields can be detected by an increasingly sophisticated array of scientific instruments which are revealing the profound activities which are the basis for our mental processes and ultimately for everything.

For many years attention regarding the underlying processes has focused on the membrane characteristics of neurons as the basis for their functions. However, recently there has been evidence that there is activity at an unexpectedly fundamental level.

Quantum processes have been predicted and observed under physiological conditions in *photosynthesis* and olfactory centers ... and very recently in microtubules, which are highly concentrated and organized inside neurons. If these quantum effects prove to be involved in cognition we will have established a direct relationship between the *human heart* and the most fundamental laws of the universe. These effects could validate some of the links which have been intimated between us and nature for millennia.

Did you know the human heart has an energy field 5,000 times greater than that of the human brain and this energy field can be measured up to 10 feet beyond the human body?

This enlightening information provides support for the spiritual teachings that indicate we human beings have energy fields that constantly intermingle with each other; which enable *thoughts* to be extended and exchanged amongst each other.

Therefore, if our thoughts were more in tune with the nature of love our brains would relay this divine energy to our hearts. And this *thoughtful* expression of love would have a profound effect on the brain's cognizant functions and intuitive clarity, along with increased feelings of well-being.

This welcomed state of balance, or coherence, between the brain and the heart will eliminate stress and will in turn open the door to *personal creativity,* as well as open the gateway to a *'peace' of subconscious mind.*

Question: Do you believe that the human heart automatically 'vibrates' on its own without any 'outside' assistance?

Well, according to scientists the sinoatrial node is a group of specialized cardiomyocytes that are innervated by feedback from the parasympathetic and sympathetic nervous system fibers and determines the rhythm within the human heart.

So, let's take a closer look at the sinoatrial node:

In the upper part of the right atrium of the heart is a group of specialized cardiomyocytes known as the sinoatrial node *(SA node).* The sinoatrial node acts as the heart's pacemaker, the SA node fires at regular intervals to cause the heart to beat with a rhythm of about 60 to 70 beats per minute. The *electrical impulse from the SA node* triggers a sequence of electrical events within the heart to control the orderly sequence of muscle contractions that pump the blood through the heart.

While it is normal for nerve cells to rely on a certain *stimulus* to fire, the SA node is presumed to be *self-firing.* Well, the way I perceive it, every cell within any machine (the SA node in this case) requires an external source of power to function (generate action potentials at the appropriate frequency) and the *human machine* is no different.

Although, the sinoatrial node may not require support from any other *internal* cells in order to operate, this certainly does not mean that it (like all other cells) is not dependent upon an essential *outside source of power.*

See the *conscious electromagnetic energy from this Universe* that we inhale every second of our existence is what sparks this seemingly automatic cell. Hence, if we stop breathing, the SA node, and all other living cells in our bodies will lose functionality and die.

What does the human heart have to do with neuro feedback?

When most people address the term *neuro*, they think neurologist, neurology, neurosurgery, etc. Thus, when you think of 'neuro' you automatically relate this to the nervous system and especially the human brain and human spinal cord; otherwise known as the central nervous system.

What does the human heart have to do with the nervous system?

Well, *our heart has its own independent nervous system*; therefore, even if our heart was disconnected from our brain, our heart would keep on *vibrating*; however that's really just the beginning. Consider the fact that the human heart is not just a pump pushing blood throughout the human body. Our heart is a highly complex, self-organized information-processing center that is communicating with and influencing the human brain by way of other parts of the nervous and hormonal system.

In fact, the heart's built-in brain is so complex that it often acts independently of our well known brain and this fascinating and enlightening information has sprouted a whole new area of study called *neuro-cardiology.*

Our heart is also an endocrine gland, producing a number of hormones; many of which are the same hormones produced and used by our brain.

So, as we can clearly see, our heart is the central link between itself, our well known brain, and our body's hormonal system. In other words, our heart is the *central hub* of the human body and of the human brain.

What happens when our heart is coherent?

First, let's make a quick distinction between the human brain's emotions and the heart's feelings. It's important to understand why coherence produces all the amazing effects that it does.

The HeartMath folks make a distinction between *lower and higher emotions*:

Lower emotions are colored by the human brain's data: *past experience, future goals, attachments, conditions.* They tend to include the emotions that do not feel so good.

Higher feelings *are authentic expressions of the moment; without expectations or conditions.*

When we are generating coherence, we are spending time with the higher feelings of *compassion, appreciation, and joy.* And these are creating that special heart rate variability rhythm of 1-cycle per 10-seconds and producing the wonderful effects of the heart-brain *in sync* quality results.

So, what are the wonderful effects of the human heart and brain being in harmony with each other?

When our heart and brain are communicating with one another as designed we experience a shift in perception in regards to certain situations. We have different insights and our conscious awareness reduces our stress. We have improved immune system responses; decreased physical pain; decreased emotional distress; improved productivity; *fewer negative emotional reactions such as anger, fear, blame, etc.,* and the ability to deal more effectively with difficult situations.

Improved heart coherence creates a more harmonious subconscious mind and via this coherency there is a positive effect on *wisdom, awareness, clarity, creativity, emotional balance, and personal effectiveness.*

Chapter IX

Our heart is the most essential organ within the human body. Considering our consciousness is distributed *solely/souly* from this central location.

Once our lungs intake the energy of *consciousness;* this electromagnetic energy is then relayed to our heart and our heart then proceeds to share this universal energy with <u>every single cell</u> within our human body. Hence, this is why every single cell within the human anatomy is considered to be conscious.

Since our heart is the primary organ that initially receives consciousness via our heart's personal neuro-transmitting system, it is responsible for communicating the Universe's intelligence to our brain or *subconscious mind.*

This conscious electromagnetic energy is of course circulated throughout the entire human body by way of our blood, which is also considered to be *liquid life.*

Well, speaking of our blood; did you know that our blood is primarily water which is composed of hydrogen and oxygen and also contains hemoglobin which contains iron?

Do you know that iron is a conductor for electricity?

See, as I mentioned in the previous chapter, oxygen or consciousness is an *electron acceptor* and the hemoglobin or iron is a red protein contained within our blood which is responsible for *transporting oxygen or* **consciousness** within the blood of all vertebrates.

So, essentially our *conscious enriched blood,* with the aid of our *heart,* arteries, blood vessels, and capillaries is responsible for ensuring that the conscious electromagnetic energy of this Universe is circulated throughout our whole body. Hence, it is only the *conscious energy of this Universe* that our human forms constantly inhale that creates a *conscious soul* within our human shell.

However, since our beliefs have sold us on the idea that we are the human shell, we human beings live a life of living Hell. In other words, *we 'pay' a devilish price* for the homage that we pay to our human forms. Thus, I guess as the saying goes, *"You get what you 'pay' for."*

Did you know we reside in a vibrating Universe?

After our life is abducted by our ego, we begin to lose sight of real life. However, we must sense, although we are subconsciously secluded from real life, that life is always revealed to us and patiently waiting upon our *present attention.*

Whether you feel this or not, during every precious second of life we are surrounded by a vibration of Universal conscious energy via the spiritual air we breathe. Even the *sacred trees* are an essential part of this vibrating Universe. Take a second and try to picture our planet without any plants or trees. Try to envision how bare and *lifeless* our world would be.

Excluding the deserts and Antarctica, regardless of where we travel around our globe, we will always encounter green life. *Thus, this green life is what helps secure* **conscious life** *within humanity.*

The spiritual air we inhale, better known as oxygen or *consciousness,* is provided compliments of our foliage due to the **sol**ar process of *photosynthesis.* The tainted air we exhale, which contains carbon dioxide, is captured by our greenery and then converted back into oxygen or *consciousness,* in order to provide us with a continuous dose of spiritual fresh air.

Notice how everything seems to possess a mysterious compatibility with our abstruse existence. *Even our trees serve a 'lively' purpose towards our overall well Being.*

Humanity is encompassed by a tremendous amount of animated energy. Every human heart *embodies* a more heighten dose of this *spiritual energy*. Thus, our heart is the initial keeper of all that is sacred; *which is us!*

See, our heart is where we are first detected, because our heart is the organ that bears our ***initial*** existence.

<u>*Please allow me to explain*</u>*:*

Through every spiritual breath a pregnant mother absorbs, her conscious enriched blood—via her umbilical cord—bestows upon her embryo the *conscious energy of this Universe*. Hence, the ultrasound which is a device used to pick up *the reflections of ultrasonic pulses,* detects during inaugural creation, the *reflections of sacred life* within the mother's womb weeks before any reproduction of the human form is plausible. This mysteriously profound object of embryonic conception is the <u>*true you*</u>*!*

During early generation our human material is pending *formulation* around *our incorporeal sacred energy.* Amid this pure, miraculous, moment of essential life our physical components do not fully exist and there is *no developed brain tissue.* Life at this point is blissfully glorious and nothing else *mortally matters* outside of the *immortal energy of you.*

Hence, as a divine conscious human being, your *sacred heart,* is the organ that *initially* embraces the *Solar energy of this Universe* which is the *energy of love that shines within the heart* of every human being. And because the human heart is the first place of residence for the *Sun's electromagnetic or 'spiritual' energy*; this exemplifies why it is commonly said that the *"Spirit of Jesus"* or the *'Sun of God'* lives within the heart of every man.

Our heart is the only human organ that we witness a beat or *vibration.* And this is because our heart originally receives and contains the *Sol Vibration of this Universe.* The human heart is indeed the human body's *sole/soul* essential organ.

I know there are a lot of man-made concepts which circulate in this world and many relate to the bewilderment of the human unknown. However, if you choose to believe in another concept; please *cradle* the *real 'conception' of who you are.*

So, based upon the above mentioned I presume that it is safe to say the human heart would be empty without the 'lively' vibrating addition of the Sun/Sol.

See, whenever our heart stops *vibrating,* this is a clear indication that the Sun's energy is no longer providing the vibration of life within the human heart. Even after our brain dies our heart is still qualified to vibrate, as long as our heart is still receiving oxygen, or in other words; still receiving the *Spirit of conscious energy from the Universe's Sun.*

Do you ever wonder if our heart is truly wicked?

Some Christian scholars tend to teach us that we are born with a wicked heart; as if to insinuate our heart, which is *a special and sensitive organ,* is a little *evil monster* that was created to intentionally make us feel bad. In reality it is only *our attention* that we often hand over to our selfish man-made paradigms that makes our heart impose a wicked feeling upon our human flesh.

See, in order for our hearts to be directly responsible for our sinful behavior, we would at least need to *pay attention* to what our hearts are trying to convey.

Please understand that our sinful behavior or our immoral actions all stem from the attention that we religiously place upon our mind chatter. Please do not accuse our humble heart for our human suffering, considering we seldom allow our heart to speak.

Humanity's perpetual subconscious thinking is synonymous to us constantly listening to our man-made *selves.* And if we are frequently communicating with our**selves**, then how can there be any room to listen to the essence of whom we are? See, if we truly yearn for love, peace, and joy; then we must cease listening to our**selves** and begin to sense what we authentically desire—*which is indeed love, peace, and joy.*

What's interesting is our human brain is considered to be the most essential organ within the human body. However, nothing could be further from the truth. If our heart did not supply our brain with conscious energy, then the human brain could not maintain its existence. And the irony here is: *as it stands now, our brain suffers from receiving inadequate consciousness, therefore it tends to drive us insane.*

<u>*Please allow me to share a short personal story with you*</u>*:*

One day I was conversing with an individual in regards to the Seven Chakras: the Root Chakra, Sacral Chakra, Solar Plexus Chakra, **Heart Chakra,** Throat Chakra, Third Eye Chakra, and the Crown Chakra. And this person was adamant that the Heart Chakra was an emotional mess and if we human beings really wanted to be able to tune into our higher *self,* then this level of awareness could only be accomplished through tapping into the *Third Eye Chakra* and the *Crown Chakra,* since these two Chakras were at the top of the Chakra pyramid.

This individual also mentioned taking esoteric mind trips into other realms of reality through being connected to the Third Eye Chakra and the Crown Chakra. Well in my opinion, to label the Heart Chakra as an *"emotional mess",* I felt was pretty harsh.

And not to discredit the Third Eye Chakra and Crown Chakra in anyway, but even with these two specific Chakras being at the top of the Chakra pyramid, the Heart Chakra, which is in the *middle of this Chakra pyramid*, still remains to be in the *center of everything that we do*; even as it relates to this spiritual line up.

Hence, every aspect of our 'Being' originally stems from this central location. However, *it is only the attention that we grant to our man-made paradigm, or our 'man-made chakra', that shocks our heart and makes it an emotional mess.*

And as it relates to taking mystical mind trips into other *subconscious realms of reality,* well quite frankly, I am more concerned with the *present mind trip* that our subconscious mind is currently taking us on within this realm of reality.

Question: Despite our religious beliefs, do you know that we are all born with a pure heart? In other words, do you realize what we deem to be a bad heart is actually a byproduct of bad thoughts?

Please know there isn't a human being that is born of this sacred Planet who arrives with an *emotionally wretched heart.* Our heart becomes damaged, because we subject our awareness to rotten man-made beliefs.

It is our heart's frequency that determines how we feel about other human beings. And I am sure we have all encountered other human beings and have said to our***selves***; *"Wow, that person gave me good/bad vibes!"* When in true essence, it is not a Bad Vibe, because our heart is not created to produce a Bad Vibration.

This adverse experience is a consequence of our heart transmitting a *low vibration* which is a direct result of our paradigms repressing our awareness to the truth that rest *solely/souly* within our heart. Hence, our heart can either contain a High or Low vibrating frequency and the strength of our *heart's frequency* depends on how *frequently* we visit it. So, please stay in tune with your heart.

High Vibrating Frequency—<u>Creates</u> a love and enthusiasm for life, it creates a strong connection with the true nature of reality, which is a *unified* connection with the universe. A high vibrating frequency also creates mental clarity and the pleasurable feelings of peace, joy, and *harmony*, considering through this level of coherency you will come to know that you are one and in *tune* with the divine nature of this universe.

Low Vibrating Frequency—Is what I consider to be a *counter creation to the laws of the universe*. This means, it is '*not in accord*' with a high vibration frequency; which in turn constructs *disharmonious* emotions such as; fear, frustration, pain, worry, etc.

A low vibration frequency is a feeling of depression, a lack of energy, and a lack of love for 'self' as well as for life itself. A low vibration frequency is a disconnection from reality hence a *disunion* from the divine nature and the laws of this universe.

The following outlines the heart's highest love frequency:

528 Hz is known as the *'Miracle'* tone which brings remarkable and extraordinary changes. According to Dr. Leonard Horowitz, 528 Hz is a frequency that is central to the *"musical mathematical matrix of creation."* More than any sound previously discovered, the *"Love frequency"* resonates at the heart of everything. It connects your heart, your spiritual energy, to the spiraling reality of the universe and earth. It is an extraordinary occurrence that surpasses all known human powers, or natural forces and is ascribed to a divine cause.

Do you ever struggle with unanswered prayers?

Humanity seems to struggle with how to effectively pray. And one of the most frustrating problems we are face with, is why our prayers seem to be randomly answered? We may not realize that the majority of our prayer requests are rarely presented as a substantial need; but more often as a *man-made want*.

Please understand that our obliging source of power can *feel* the difference between whether or not our prayers are *Being* generated from our heart, or only from our man-made paradigms. Therefore, any egoist prayer petition assembled by our *man-made cravings* will be dishonored!

Our Heart's Sole (Sol) Purpose

This Universe will only be employed with answering our prayers if we *submit a heartfelt prayer application*. Hence, our answered prayers will always be based upon what we *essentially need* versus what we *egotistically want*.

Did you know there are two key performers starring in our reality show?

There are two featured performers starring in our reality show that we call *"The Mystery of Life!"*

Top billing goes to our heart which has cast us, the *soul*, with the leading role in our reality. And the supporting role goes to our brain or subconscious mind which has been billed as our *co-star*.

However, our man-made paradigms have found a treacherous way to dim the light on whom we truly are; this prevents us from shining. Now with our subconscious mind taking on a solo performance, we as the soul observers, have been downgraded to the role of an extra. We human beings must attempt to comprehend that without us *Being present* to lead our subconscious mind through life, we may have an unhappy ending with no encore.

See, the human body is comprised of two major organs; the Heart *(the initial resting place for the soul)* and the Brain or the *subconscious mind.* And between these two essential organs, *no matter* what we may think, our heart reigns supreme. Yet, the man-made rhetoric within our subconscious mind has been able to convince us otherwise.

Therefore, since we are conditioned to believe that our brain has precedence over our heart, we are more associated with our man-made beliefs versus our universal feelings. Please try to understand, as a conscious soul, despite what our paradigms may say our life's purpose is not to seek suffering.

Please understand our heart and our brain are designed to work in sync, or in harmony with each other; which means these two organs must be in proper alignment. Thus our heart which is the central location for *us*, the *soul*, has been chosen to inspire our subconscious mind with loving thoughts and through this specific synchronization we human beings will live a life of loving harmony.

However, since our attention has been disconnected from our heart, this translates into being severed from our Supreme Source of Power. Because of this separation, we human beings are left to struggle through life in turmoil as we are being controlled and manipulated by the beliefs that are stored within our subconscious minds.

Please realize that day in and day out, as we unknowingly stumble throughout life our subconscious mind controls every aspect of our behavior. This subconscious state of living means we have limited control over what we do; which clearly explains why our lives are so out of control.

In summary, the human heart is the initial home for the *shining star* of our life. Hence, we as *souls of this Universe* have been cast with the leading role to act out our reality. And every thought that we produce, paints a detailed portrait of our reality. *Therefore, we need to quit doodling with our lives and paint a masterpiece.*

Have you ever heard the following expression, "Whatever a man thinketh in his heart so is he"?

I am here to say that this statement bears no truth; considering it is not what a man thinketh in his heart; *it's what a man **thinketh upon** in his subconscious mind, so is he!*

<u>For an example</u>:

Let's say that our subconscious mind is bombarded with man-made concepts of *hate, fear, worry, etc.* Whether we realize this or not, it is actually these destructive concepts that lurk within our subconscious mind that constantly grasp our attention that has a profound effect on how our heart makes us feel. Considering, if we day in and day out, think upon the dreadful man-made data that is stored within our subconscious mind, then our heart has no choice but to make us feel and experience what we think upon most.

See, the majority of our thinking is done incoherently. However, a thought is a thought, and whether our thoughts are coherent or not, they will be the building blocks that will be used to build our reality.

Our lives are *built* from our thoughts that are generated from the information that is *built-up* in our subconscious minds. Hence, the majority of our thoughts are misguided and exploited by the arguable information that is stored within our subconscious minds.

The vast majority of our thoughts, on a daily basis, are thoughts that are based upon inconclusive beliefs. These thoughts are incoherent or *subconscious thoughts*, which translate to living a life of uncertainty.

Although our heart is a physical organ which is designed to make us feel glorious, it's our incoherent thoughts that *linger* upon our beliefs that make our heart stimulate anguish.

Therefore, as we proceed through life *unfocused,* this lack of coherency plagues us with uncertainty. Hence Jesus' expression, *"Forgive them Father for they know not what they do"* (Luke 23:34).

This ultimately means if we change the direction of what we dwell upon most, we will in turn change how our heart makes us feel. Thus, in most cases, the life we live is not the life we truly desire; *but often the life we unknowingly worry about.*

Why do we choose to feel bad if we are created to feel Divine?

The emotional hurricanes we human beings experience in life are only linked to our beliefs. And since we do not possess coherent control of where our thoughts dwell, we are not capable of controlling our emotions.

We may think we act upon our true feelings, but this is only based upon what we have been conditioned to believe. We are seldom inspired to act upon how we really feel. In other words, we rarely do what we *feel* is right, because we often do what we *subconsciously think* is right. And subconscious communication will always leave us with a sense of anxiety, as it compares to not being conscious of the truth.

Intuition from this Universe is presented in the essence of a *strong congruent feeling.* And a congruent feeling is a feeling that creates harmony within our human form. Therefore, any feeling that clash with harmony should be deemed as an *incongruent emotion.*

Now, intuition from the Universe is a *feeling* that is always granted to us between our lower chest and our diaphragm, which we ordinarily refer to as a *"gut feeling"*. Another name for this *enlightening* internal location is ironically called the *"**Solar Plexus**"*.

This *heartfelt feeling* is a universal impulse to do what is right. However, since the melody within our subconscious mind proceeds to play the same old songs we continue to dance through life all wrong.

Since we mainly identify with the man-made doctrine that is embedded within our subconscious mind we tend to experience subconscious emotions. A subconscious mind that is empty of a conscious loving heart is not designed to provide us with a true loving feeling.

Therefore, a subconscious mind that is without a lucid heart, can only supply the human form with *Emotions that are filled with distress* such as; *Hate, Fear, Greed, Envy, Jealousy, Worry, etc.* Do any of these *subconscious emotions* feel familiar?

Our Heart's Sole (Sol) Purpose

Do you realize that our dark man-made paradigms have eclipsed the light of our awareness?

Do you know as divine human beings we are born to consciously 'love' before we are subconsciously taught to 'hate'?

As I have mentioned throughout this book, our human suffering is primarily based upon the *beliefs* which conceal the treasure that shines within our heart. We will never see the *light of reality* if we continue to be sheltered by the shadow of darkness that currently occupies our subconscious mind. Thus, please cease believing our heart is responsible for the evil that our man-made convictions are *responsible* for.

By way of our conditioning we live a selfish and subpar life. Hence, through our man-made conditioning we are *automatically driven* to *selfishly* exist through a controversial world composed of a debatable reality versus being a *soulful* part of a harmonious world that is based upon true reality. Thus, it becomes difficult to see our way when the window to our awareness is distorted by conflicting beliefs.

We human beings need to cease *subconsciously existing* in an obscure man-made world filled with troublesome and misleading artifacts and start *consciously living* in a world where authentic life really *matters*.

Do you believe our hearts are the doorway to Heaven?

Do you realize that Heaven is a 'feeling' and not really a place?

Please embrace the following information, because it outlines how our **Heart**s contain the sacred key to the doorway of **Heaven**—which leads to *your divine nature.*

As Jesus said, "*The Kingdom of Heaven lives within you!*" In other words, man's version of Heaven that we are *dying* to get to is actually nothing more than a *divine feeling* that is *born* within the heart of every human being."

Chapter IX

The human heart contains the answers to all we seek. And only through becoming fully 'aware' that you are the divine soul *that represents the energy of conscious life* within your human form, will you know exactly what this Universe has in store for you.

Please understand our heart is far more valuable than we have been conditioned to believe. The true divine purpose of our heart is to work in conscious cooperation with our brain by allowing us the *solar energy* within our human form to feel what it is like to behave in a coherent manner with life.

We human beings must someday acknowledge that our human forms, as well as our human brain, are both *lifeless* without the conscious inclusion of this Universe. However, since our beliefs that dwell within our subconscious mind have made us unaware of this truth, this vague awareness has in a sense destroyed our lives.

Until we realize that we are far more than what we see, we will never be free. We human beings will always be *slaves* to our beliefs as long as our subconscious minds are *separated* from the *love of this Universe* that originally shines within our hearts.

The key is to free our awareness from our man-made beliefs that are shackled to our minds by shifting our awareness towards our **Hearts**. And once we insert the *key of awareness* into the door that grants access into our hearts we will then behold that our hearts are the only true doorways to **Heaven**.

Once we become aware that the human *chest* contains the greatest *treasure* currently unknown to man we will recognize that we have discovered the glorious *Treasure Chest* that we have all been seeking since the beginning of our existence. This glorious awakening will re-direct our awareness to a true sense of knowing; trust me there is no better feeling than knowing the *God's honest truth*.

Until we human beings awaken and realize that the *'light of love'* from the Universe's Sun shines within our hearts we human beings will never be "*lighthearted.*"

Do you know what I find intriguing? We human beings battle every single day (heck every single second) with not knowing who we really are and what our 'sole/soul' purpose for being here is.

And yet, even in the midst of this profound absence of knowing, we still believe that we are the smartest species on the planet.

We human beings dash through life thinking that we are so smart; however, we fail to do our true part, because we toss everyone else's ideas and beliefs into our own conviction cart.

We human beings must learn, that the genuine truth can only be realized, once we open our subconscious minds to our hearts; since only through this access can true enlightenment be sparked.

We human beings have grown to be so *devilishly* smart that we have become oblivious to our own *divine* nature. See, whether we human beings acknowledge this or not, our intelligence is all relative. Since we do not utilize or maximize our true *conscious potential* like other conscious life forms, we may indeed be the least intelligent creatures on this planet.

Do you know wisdom is a blessing that can never be taught, it can only be discovered?

We human beings must make a conscious effort to tap into our hearts and open our subconscious minds in order to be granted with the gift of divine wisdom. But first we need to slam the door that leads to our manipulating man-made paradigm and stop *lending our attention* to our man-made beliefs, because quite frankly we can't *afford* to give it. Thus, as the saying goes, *"Do not lend what you cannot afford to give."*

X

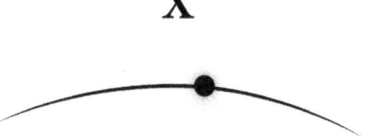

The Man-Made Mind

Our subconscious minds are gifts from this Universe. However, the subconscious mind of each and every soul has been transformed into a mind that has been reformed by man because of the man-made theories, ideas, philosophies, etc., which have infiltrated and infected our subconscious minds. And since our subconscious minds have been corrupted by man's beliefs, they have now become *"man-made minds."*

Here are two of the most common questions asked in regards to the human brain:

1. What makes up the human brain?

2. How powerful is the human brain?

However, the most 'crucial' question we need to ask is: How 'self-controlling' is the human brain or the subconscious mind?

I know according to Sigmund Freud's theory we presumably have *three separate* or different levels to our mind; *the conscious mind, the preconscious mind, and the unconscious mind.* Some believe our conscious mind, *which of course has yet to be well defined*, is what most people associate with in order to define who they are.

Although, as I addressed in a prior chapter, until someone is capable of unveiling a *so called conscious mind* we human beings do not possess one. Considering, the *soul or the spirit* of who we are is what represents the *conscious observer.*

Furthermore, as I mentioned at the very beginning of this book, we are born *pure in **mind**, pure in body, and pure in soul.* Thus, we do not even have a *pre-conscious* or *unconscious* mind, assuming the **mind** *is not plural!* Hence, from my insight, we human beings only occupy **one** mind. And this one mind is the *Almighty Subconscious Mind.*

The human subconscious is poorly understood, but thought to be more powerful than our most advanced computers, especially in areas such as innovation, understanding, and pattern recognition. No man-made machine or system in this world can rival the brain in its specialties.

And as a wise man once said, "With great power, comes great responsibility!"

So, imagine if you will this type of power in the wrong hands. Imagine what it would be like relinquishing your subconscious mind or your power to the hands of another person?

Whether we realize this or not, every day that we rely on our beliefs, in order to determine the meaning of life, this Universe, or who we truly are, we have in essence, placed our lives in someone else's hands. Because these ideas and beliefs that we all live by, have been 'buried' in our minds by someone else.

The human brain controls memory, vision, learning, *processes our thoughts, and our awareness* among other numerous behind the scenes *(seen)* activities.

During fetal development the foundations of the human brain are laid as billions of neurons forming trillions of appropriate connections and patterns. No aspect of this complicated structure has been left to chance. The scheme for the wiring plan is encoded in the genes. It has been shown from previous studies that in developing embryos of animals, nerve cells travel to designated regions of the brain, and once in place send out axons along pre-programmed paths to make contact with specific targets.

The brain's 86 billion neurons connect with one another in complex networks. All physical and mental functioning depend on the establishment and maintenance of neural networks which connect each neuron which is a complex structure of electrochemical components. A person's habits and skills, such as nail-biting or playing a musical instrument become embedded within the human brain or subconscious mind in frequently activated neural networks. When a person stops performing an activity, the neural networks for the activity fall into disuse.

The human brain works feverishly behind the scenes regulating everything from breathing to mate selection. In fact, neuroscientist David Eagleman of Baylor College of Medicine argues that the non-conscious workings of the human brain are so crucial to everyday functioning that their influence often *trumps conscious thought*. To prove it, he explores little-known historical episodes, the latest psychological research, and enduring medical mysteries, revealing the bizarre and often inexplicable mechanisms underlying daily life.

Eagleman's theory is epitomized by the deathbed revelation of the 19th-century mathematician James Clerk Maxwell, who developed the fundamental equations unifying *electricity and magnetism*. Maxwell declared that *something within him* had made the discoveries, and that he actually had no idea how he had achieved his great insights. It is easy to take credit after an idea strikes you, but in fact, neurons in your brain secretly perform an enormous amount of work before *'inspiration'* hits. The human brain, Eagleman argues, runs its *'own'* show incognito or as Pink Floyd said, *"There's someone in my head; but it's not me."*

So out of curiosity, do you ever wonder why certain dreams, feel so real?

Well, even as we rest, the energy of this Universe is circulating throughout our human framework and providing our brain with the energy of consciousness, which manifest into visions of subconscious awareness. Thus, even our dreams and nightmares, which are *subconscious illusions,* often *feel real.*

Do you know why it is said that we human beings at 'most' use approximately 5% of our brain capacity?

Well, that's because the other 95% of our brain uses us!

Hence, we are robotically being controlled by the man-made concepts lying active within our brain. In other words, 95% of our behavior, actions, and even our perceptions, are *automatically* being triggered by the beliefs that lay festering within our subconscious minds.

<u>Here's what I mean</u>:

Every single day of our lives we meander through the present moment with only a vague sense of what truly defines the meaning of life. Considering, a vast majority of our awareness is being held hostage by our mind which provides us with the definition of a victimized life. Therefore, we lack the ability to embrace the authenticity of life in the manner in which it should be experienced.

<u>Here is an example as to why most of humanity has no real idea how reality feels</u>:

Although we are always *physically* residing within the present moment, 95% of our incoherent awareness is centered on dwelling upon *our past failures and worrying about our future wants.* And only 5% of our coherent attention is *vaguely* placed upon what is happening within the present moment. Therefore, life within this special moment, due to our limited awareness, appears to be dreadfully overcast and hazy.

If we really take the time to notice this incoherency of the present moment we will discover that we never possess a vivid perception of reality.

Once your full attention is relinquished to the present moment, the beauty of life becomes crystal clear. Although, while you are granting your attention to the present moment, please try to *observe* and accept the moment for what is, versus perceiving it from a man-made concept.

Considering, the moment we start *thinking* about what is transpiring within the present moment, whether we recognize this or not, we have gone from consciously *appreciating* the moment to subconsciously *judging* it, through our man-made perception of life.

Do you see why our man-made beliefs are so controlling?

It's because we never question or give our beliefs a second thought.

See, our problem is we *believe in so much,* yet we still *know nothing.* Which means our subconscious mind is filled with man's *judgmental 'beliefs'* and completely absent of *'knowing' the Universal Truth.*

Although experts have yet to determine the nature of our thoughts, they presume that some part of our brain is actually producing our thoughts. However, once we ascertain the true origin of our thoughts, we will realize that our brain does not directly produce our thoughts; our brain in fact only *processes* the meaning of our thoughts. And in addition to processing our thoughts, our brain also determines our *perception.* Thus, as I mentioned in an earlier chapter, as an *untouchable* conscious Being you are the producer of an *intangible* thought.

Chapter X

The real truth of the matter is our brain or subconscious mind requires the *electromagnetic* energy of our *thoughts* in order to function. In other words, our brain/subconscious mind relies on our thoughts and our awareness *which are generated from our conscious energy* in order to thrive and survive.

However, due to the 'unawareness' of our own power our subconscious mind 'misuses' our conscious energy in order to govern and rule our lives.

Our ego which governs our subconscious mind, feeds off of our conscious energy in order to maintain its existence. It manipulates our incoherent thoughts and exploits our awareness, in order to create our synthetic reality. In other words, our *ego* needs us more than we need it in order to stay alive.

Our subconscious mind is designed to regulate and not create without our conscious control. And because our subconscious mind is trying to be constructive without our conscious guidance our human form tends to malfunction.

As I mentioned above, even as powerful as our subconscious mind is, 'It' is powerless without our conscious spirit. Therefore, do you know that our subconscious mind is created to be a servant to our consciousness; hence the prefix, 'Sub'?

<u>Please make an effort to grasp the following</u>:

Our *sub*-conscious mind is designed to be a *sub*-product of our consciousness. And our *sub*-conscious mind is also created to obey or be *sub*-ordinate to our consciousness.

However, here is something that I find fascinating. Although our consciousness is actually supposed to be *sub*-jective to our *sub*-conscious mind, since this Almighty tool never came with an *instruction manual* on how to properly utilize it; *it has in turn* **sub**-*jected us to 'Being' its* **sub**-*ordinate.*

The Man-Made Mind

<u>*Here is an animated example of what I mean*</u>:

We human beings are prisoners within our own subconscious minds, caged within a quarantined mental cell and our *egos are the controlling Warden(s)* that are constantly making all the rules. We must do a lot of soul searching, in order to free ourselves from this mental prison or else we, as *Souls of this Universe,* will spend *life sentences* in this *self-assigned* Hell hole.

It's amazing how we human beings persistently fight to maintain our physical freedom, yet we fail to acknowledge that our <u>*awareness is enslaved*</u> by our own mind.

We all need to face the reality of knowing that true freedom can only be granted by way of our attention being released from the shackles that are attached to our own subconscious minds.

As I have mentioned in an earlier chapter, the only reason we are held *captive* by our subconscious minds, is because we are frequently *captivated* by our man-made beliefs. Our subconscious mind is also like the Land of OZ and our Ego is the Grand Wizard. Considering we have yet to define who we are, our *man-made image* is a collection of many different identities. Hence, we are comprised of all the cast members in this *illusionary* movie.

Thus, we are like Dorothy, trapped in this wicked mysterious world wanting to find our way back home. We are also like the Tin Man, the Scarecrow, and of course the *Cowardly Lion*. We are drenched with *fear* as we travel along this man-made brick road of misery. And as it relates to us being similar to the Tin Man and the Scarecrow, because we do not use our *heart* and our *brain* in the manner in which they were created, it's like neither of these essential components exist.

We actually need to be more like Dorothy and find us a pair of ruby slippers and click our heels three times and say, *"There is no place like home."* Why? *Because home is where the heart is!*

Chapter X

Did you know the two primary roles of our subconscious mind are to Protect and Serve?

Our subconscious mind is designed to be used in a prudent manner. It is constructed to *protect* us by all means necessary and to *serve* us with whatever we desire through our *emotional thoughts*.

See, our subconscious mind responds only to what we feed it, by way of consistent thought. And after our subconscious mind stores a regularly thought upon belief as being valid, this automatically forms what we call *our second nature*. Hence, anything that we *religiously* dwell upon, over-and-over-again, our subconscious mind will eventually alleviate us from having to consciously focus on these specific actions and beliefs. Thus, these human behaviors will automatically become part of our everyday life without a *second thought*.

I really feel humanity (for the most part) has no Earthly idea how much power we possess by way of our subconscious mind. Our subconscious mind is an outlet for our power; considering whatever we thoughtfully feed to our subconscious mind, our subconscious mind will digest our emotional input and proceed to *serve* us with whatever we coherently or incoherently ordered.

However, there is a caveat to being connected to this much power. Our subconscious mind is *extremely obedient* and it is equipped to obey our every command, via thought; without any questions asked. In other words, our subconscious mind is not going to attempt to correct us, negotiate with us, or even determine whether or not certain information that we choose to dwell upon is *helpful* or *harmful*.

Therefore, if you have accepted something or anything as being your concept of the truth, well then your subconscious mind will ensure that you experience what you have deemed to be legitimate. And once your subconscious mind *serves* you with what you have *thought* to be credible, it will then proceed to *protect* your chosen belief by all means necessary.

You may be wondering how in the world did we lose complete control of our subconscious minds?

The simple answer is we have yet to distinguish the massive difference between *reality* and *non-reality*. Now, I am sure you have heard of the common expression, *peace of mind*. Well, our subconscious mind can only provide us with a *feeling* of *peace* when our awareness is bestowed upon the true nature of reality.

However, if we take the time to become aware of our awareness we will detect that we are way too busy to be bothered with the presence of reality. Considering we are too pre-occupied living within a world of non-reality by way of being eagerly employed by our man-made beliefs.

Thus, we are in turn desperately trying to cope with the enormous amount of anxiety and stress that is constantly occupying our awareness, through the dedicated attention that we grant to unrealistic time—*otherwise known as the past and the future.*

Let me ask you a very important question and please try to grant this question your undivided attention. When you awake in the morning and you are introduced to a 'new' day, what do you immediately do?

In other words, after you are granted with another 'enlightening' day to explore, experience, and enjoy do you promptly tap into the presence of this glorious day or do you 'automatically' focus on what happen yesterday and what you expect to unfold tomorrow?

I am willing to bet my life, that nine times out of ten, you are instantly plugging into your subconscious mind and *thinking about yesterday and concerning your-self with tomorrow*. Do you happen to sense that every precious moment of *existing life* that we choose to ignore in order to waste our attention within our subconscious mind that bears *no real existence* we are actually manifesting our own human suffering?

Chapter X

We suffer from shunning reality to live within a man-made world that exists within our subconscious mind where official reality is not present. Considering there is *nothing* transpiring within our subconscious mind that is *genuinely* taking place within the present moment.

In other words, there is no point in time while our attention is residing within our subconscious world that we are capable of *physically* interacting with the man-made mayhem that is parading around throughout our subconscious minds.

Yet, via our attention we spend our entire lives within this man-made world of make believe.

So, in order to find true peace within our human form we must make sure that our *attention is still.* However, I do not mean still focusing on the past and the future; I mean completely *still* and *fastened* to *life* which only resides within the present moment.

Question: *If our subconscious mind does not require our awareness in order to perform its designated or routine duties, then why do we lend so much of our attention to it?*

The subconscious mind carries out its everyday duties without having to be supervised. Although, based upon the current state of our subconscious mind it really needs to be micro-managed.

<u>Here are some of the subconscious mind's primary duties</u>:

The subconscious mind regulates all human bodily functions, automatically controls breathing, *stores conscious memories*, and also *controls human behavior.* The subconscious mind also strives to protect human beings from harm and danger.

However, our subconscious mind was not designed to control or manipulate a human being's consciousness. Our subconscious mind is created to be susceptible to our conscious encounters and then our subconscious mind proceeds to build upon our life experiences. Hence, our subconscious mind is constructed to *automatically* determine our *perception of life* based upon the *reality* that we have passionately accepted.

We habitually dwell upon a man-made form of reality; this unawareness of the true *nature* of reality, bestows upon our subconscious mind a disturbing concept of life. Thus, our poorly programmed subconscious mind proceeds to function accordingly.

Hence, this improper wiring creates an inadequate human behavior which often results in human havoc. And due to our blindness of our divine nature, it also seems as if our subconscious mind, or our man-made mind, has picked up on this *absent mindedness* or *absent awareness* and decided to take full control of our lives.

<u>*Here's an animated analogy of what I am referring to:*</u>

It appears that we human beings are oblivious to the fact that we are *conscious Beings* who have been created to *consciously love and appreciate life based upon an authentic reality.* Since we have become reliant upon our *mind* for guidance, our mind has in turn become arrogant and rebellious. Thus, we have been misguided and manipulated into using *man-made concepts, in order to live a life that is based upon a deceptive reality.*

In light of our subconscious mind's demanding mundane duties such as regulation of our bodily functions and storing memories, our subconscious mind through its new found pseudo sense of power is offended by being relegated to the subordinate tasks of maintaining our *routine bodily functions.*

Therefore, our mind *thought* it should be promoted to govern our thoughts—especially since we do not appear to be *present.* So based upon our unawareness of our own divine nature, our mind figured it would go *ahead,* and take over our lives.

This is not our subconscious mind's legitimate role, but without our conscious supervision our subconscious mind has been performing miserably and we human beings are a direct byproduct of this man-made misery.

Due to the fact that our subconscious minds should not be in *total control* of our lives; we have allowed our subconscious minds, via our man-made perceptions of life, to construct for us lives that are filled with distress and self-destruction.

See, in the *absence of 'Being' aware of our own awareness,* our subconscious mind can only manifest artificial intelligence, which displays an inferior perception of *who we are.*

As I have stated above, our subconscious minds are designed to *regulate and not create* without our awareness. And since our subconscious minds are attempting to be creative on their own, they are not operating in conjunction with Universal Law. Therefore, the human body tends to be impaired under the struggling independence of our mind's *selfish* desire to create.

Universal laws have, and will always, exist since they determine processes of creation, manifestation, and management of the universe. Nothing is made randomly. Everything is governed by perfect laws. Even though we may not understand or be familiar with them, we are permanently experiencing them and can verify their presence in all events manifested around us.

Different from the laws of men, which change continuously depending on circumstances, universal laws are immutable principles that provide the origin and the perfect order of everything in the universe.

As we move forward in our development of consciousness, we discover processes that free us from the constraints of Man's ego and align us with the perfect order. However, a mind full of ideas, concepts, and beliefs resists, opposes, and refuses to understand the principles of the Universe.

It seems that, based upon the ample amount of power that our subconscious minds are capable of they have constructed *synthetic lives of their own, by way of leveraging the beliefs that they have accumulated.* And since we fail to tap into the present realm of a *'Wholly'* reality, our minds have been able to capture and steer our attention towards a *divisive* reality which is a world where we as *conscious* children of this Universe have no *'self'* control.

Now we are trapped within this make believe world created by our minds. Through this imprisonment our subconscious minds have discovered how much power they have acquired. And not only through being able to automatically control the human form's physical mechanics, but also how they are capable of *spontaneously* governing our behavior and actions through manipulating our awareness.

This invasion or acquisition of our awareness has amplified our minds' concocted sense of control. And through this *Self-Made Power Trip,* our subconscious mind has developed a *Selfish Man-Made Ego which is custom designed to exploit our thoughts and awareness.*

Please understand our subconscious mind is a *sacred gift* from this Universe and there is absolutely nothing that can compete with its supreme power. Therefore, if we ever determine how to use our subconscious mind in a coherent manner it can be the most rewarding *present* that we have ever received. However, since we human beings have yet to comprehend how to successfully operate this glorious gift, we fail to properly function and achieve our full potential.

So, considering we have yet to consciously unveil *who we are,* this critical unawareness has left us yet to discover how to control our subconscious minds. And since this understanding has yet to come to fruition our subconscious mind has, in the interim, discovered how to harmfully influence us.

Chapter X

As, I stated above, humanity really needs to take some time and do some real *soul searching* in order to unravel the mechanics of our subconscious mind, as we would any other *'malfunctioning'* device. Considering in our Earthly lifetimes there is nothing that will ever *matter* more.

We human beings must awaken to the fact that our subconscious minds are an Almighty instrument that is considered to be our possession. Therefore we need to cease allowing it to possess us.

Once we learn how to effectively manage our subconscious minds we will then be promoted to C.E.O. of our own lives. Though, if we continue to be employed by our man-made E.G.O.s, then we will forever be their hard working employees.

Now with all this being said, you may be curious to know that if all this information is indeed true, then why is most of humanity so oblivious to it?

Well, the simple answer is it's hard to see the forest for the trees. Or in other words, *"It's hard to see the 'soul' truth for the man-made lies."*

<u>Here are four profound reasons as to why most of humanity is not aware of the truth that defines our divine nature</u>:

1. We are seeking the *truth* within a domain that is primarily filled with man-made *lies*. Our subconscious minds do not have the answer to who we really are, because our subconscious minds have never been provided with the *essential* information.

2. Since we have never been aware of the internal truth which defines us as loving human beings, this lack of awareness means that our subconscious mind has never been *formally* introduced to our divine nature.

Since our subconscious minds have no Earthly idea what genuinely defines our nature it is not equipped to relay this vital information back to us. In other words, our subconscious minds were not created to provide us with an answer; that, quite frankly, we as *conscious souls* should *naturally* know.

Therefore, even using a search light for whom we are within the current dark parameters of our subconscious minds will still leave us without an understanding. Thus, we can never be *enlightened to the truth* if we reside within the darkness of our subconscious minds. Our attention is usually spent *outside of a loving reality*; considering we waste our entire lives spending our awareness *inside our subconscious minds focusing on a dreadful reality* which consists of man-made concepts and ideas that form our disgruntled lives.

3. Our subconscious minds can only provide us with what we furnish them by way of what we believe. Therefore, if we supply our subconscious minds with selfish and destructive beliefs, then our subconscious minds will accommodate us with selfish and destructive lifestyles.

Unfortunately, our *subconscious* minds are not employed to know how terrible our thoughts or beliefs make us feel. And the real reason we encounter fear and worry is because we spend our entire lives reflecting upon a *man-made world* that is filled with despair.

4. Our egos are very defensive and hell bent on preventing changes, because they have worked extremely hard to ensure and *reinforce* our existing beliefs.

Therefore, the moment we try to *feel* something outside of our existing paradigm, our egos are simply not going to allow that. Hence, this is why any attempt towards changing our paradigms is so difficult.

So, based upon our current state of mind, if we continue to refer to our *mind*, for the *'soul'* truth; then unfortunately our subconscious mind has no choice but to *lie* to us.

Chapter X

Without our conscious input, our subconscious minds are in no way privy to this level of knowing. Hence, if the divinity of this Universe is never introduced to our subconscious minds, then we will forever be *"absent minded!"*

Question, do you believe whenever you administer a prayer to your religious version of this Universe, (specifically by name); your elected idea of this Universe is the 'one' and 'only' entity that is responsible for answering your prayers?

Well, if your answer is yes, do you understand that the energy of love, which defines this Universe, really has no man-made name? In other words, do you know that the loving essence of who we are was theoretically born with no name? And that the naming of every human being is nothing more than a man-made concept used as a recognition label to identify our man-made self?

<u>Here is what I am really trying to convey</u>:

Whenever we pray to our religious versions of this Universe by their *man-made names*, despite what we have been convinced to believe, these *man-made symbols of this Universe* that we are *worshipping and praying to in reality do not exist.*

In other words, the Religious Gods that we personally worship *specifically by name*, are nothing more than figments of our man-made imagination.

As mentioned earlier in this chapter we human beings have no Earthly idea how much power we possess via our subconscious minds.

See, the only entity that is actually responding to our prayer requests is our *Subconscious Mind.* Beneath the human flesh, we are all divine conscious Beings and our subconscious minds are powerful tools that are designed to help manifest whatever we desire while within this realm of reality.

In other words, the primary duty of our subconscious mind is to assist with *honoring all of our beliefs*, regardless if they are *deceptive* or not.

In truth, it is our *unawareness of how much power is packed into a belief,* which makes even the most *unrealistic beliefs* seem so real. Hence, the only reason our beliefs feel so real is because we don't *know* that it is only our energy that we bundle into a conviction that brings a man-made belief to life.

With this being said, please allow me to ask 'you' a very meaningful question and please try to be honest with your 'self'.

If you strongly believe in your religious version of this Universe, then please ask your 'self' this very sincere question; out of every single belief that you hold dear to your heart, is there a belief that can actually rival your religious belief?

I am not a betting man; however, if I had to gamble on this one all my chips would be on the table.

If we have formed a strong love and adoration for our religious version of this Universe, then every other belief within our man-made paradigm will actually pale in comparison to our religious belief. Hence, the more energy we put forth towards a belief, the more effort and energy our subconscious mind will exude in order to make sure this belief *seems real*.

Therefore, I feel that it is safe to say if our religious belief rules our paradigm, then we have *sacrificed our entire life* to man's concept of religion. Which means we have *relinquished all of our spiritual power* to a **'theoretical idea'** of this Universe; *which in turn makes us believe that this idea is real!*

Thus, I ask you this very profound question, If your 'feeling' for man's idea of this Universe is more profound than the love you have for yourself, your parents, your spouse, and even your

Chapter X

children, then wouldn't your Religious notion of this Universe 'feel' very real?

See, if our *man-made version* of this Universe is the most important figure in our life and there is nothing that we love or *believe in more;* well then, this *profound belief* will equate to a *profound feeling* which will make our belief seem very real. Hence, our *'reality'* will always be based upon what we believe in most. Or in other words, whatever *we experience in life* will consistently be based upon what we believe in.

Before we proceed to further discuss Man's version of this Universe, I do have an essential question for you; is it safe to say that every human being that resides on planet Earth consumes the exact same Air?

Okay, so if every Earthling shares the same air which is distributed by the Sun, which in turn grants us 'eternal' life, then this should help us to envision that if we all absorb the same solar or conscious energy through the Sun, then the 'Sol' of this Universe must be what defines us all. Thus, we all rely on the same source of conscious energy that is lavished from the 'Sol' of 'One' Universe.

Every single breath we take of solar energy is laced with electro-*magnetic* energy and, yes, I am placing much emphasis on the word **magnetic**. See, the measure of faith that we employ to support our prayers will determine the level of *electro-magnetic energy* that will be utilized to *fuel our emotional requests*. And if our *faith is strong,* then this *powerful emotion* will be the *soul* catalyst towards **magnetically attracting** the answers to our prayers.

So, since we all contain and are united with the conscious electro-*magnetic* energy of this Universe, the moment this *electro-magnetic* energy is transmitted to our subconscious mind via a *thought and/or emotion,* this magnetic energy is what motivates our subconscious mind to seek and *magnetically draw* a similar energy to satisfy our prayers.

We human beings are all linked to the same source of *electromagnetic* energy; heck this entire Universe is connected and held together by this same source of spiritual energy. Therefore in reality, we will never draw what we casually want out of life, since there is no *real emotion* associated with these weak desires. However, based upon the magnitude of our invested emotions, we are practically guaranteed a *Heavenly* or *Hellish* return.

Do you ever wonder if our religious version of this Universe is an illusion?

Well in reality, the religious Gods that we are conditioned to pray to are nothing more than man-made illusions. See, as I mentioned above, our subconscious mind responds only to the *energy* that we feed it. And it is only our thoughts and emotions that drive our subconscious mind towards claiming our prayers.

In other words, our subconscious mind does not respond to the magnitude of any *name request,* it is only *inspired* to answer our desires based upon the extent of our *emotional request.* Hence, our subconscious mind is a divine gift from this Universe that is created to serve and feed our *emotional appetite* and was never designed to honor the names of any man-made concepts of this Universe. Therefore, our love should only be directed towards a divine *Universal energy* that bears no man-made name.

Although, with us being unaware of the divine power that we possess, our *mind* makes us believe that our religious version of this Universe is indeed the *prime administer* backing our prayers. Hence, the moment we utter the names: *dear Lord Jesus, dear Allah, dear Buddha, dear Jehovah,* etc., our religious fantasy is promptly triggered. And if our prayers are granted, then our religious version of God receives all the glory. This means we have now *reinforced* our religious belief that our man-made idea of this Universe is indeed the real deal. It is through this delusionary process that diverse religious believers believe that their religious concept of this Universe is *exclusively the One!*

Chapter X

This brings me to my next question. Do you realize the culture we are born into defines the religious version of this Universe that we will be conditioned to worship?

Honestly, I do not sense there's a human being on this planet that feels their culture does not define them. There is no stronger influence than our cultures, which are present all day, every day of our lives. Hence our elected religions and our cultures that we are born into are indeed one in the same.

The religion we "choose" to worship is embedded in our cultural beliefs. The religious Gods that we have been conditioned to worship do not serve as a sacred truth; they only represent our daily cultural reality.

Hence, do you know the beliefs that we relinquish to our religion(s) are not a fair trade?

See, the energy that we invest in our religions is far more valuable than the false hopes that our religions provide us.

As I mentioned earlier, energy is the force behind everything we do and it is only the energy that we plug into our religious beliefs that is used to fuel our religions. This makes our religions a formidable force to be reckoned with.

It is undeniably the collective energy of every religious believer that is the *'manpower' that grants their religion immeasurable power.* This is why religion is constantly seeking *new souls* to suck the *life* out of.

<u>Please allow me to share a brief story with you</u>:

One day someone inquired if I had ever encountered demons or evil spirits and I simply replied, *"No."* Then I in turn asked them the same question and their response was adamantly, *"Yes!"*

So I asked, well if you have experienced demons or evil spirits, I guess it's safe to say that you actually *believe* in such a thing? And they replied, *"Of course!"*

Then I said, "Well, with that being stated, I am sure that I will never encounter any demons or evil spirits." They replied, *"What makes you so sure?"* I said *"Well, because I do not believe in such things."*

The moral of this story is, whatever you believe in most, you will achieve with the persistent help of your subconscious mind. Hence, as the saying goes; *"Believe and you shall achieve."* In other words, *our prayers are not granted based upon the religious Gods that we believe in; our prayers are only answered because we simply believe!*

Thus, it is only the level of energy that we expend that is ultimately responsible for manifesting what we choose to believe is real.

Did you know that the power of our ego only rests within our subconscious mind?

Even though our *ego* is extremely powerful, please know its power is only limited to our *subconscious reality*. And since we spend the bulk of our lives within our subconscious mind via our misguided awareness we *religiously* allow our egos to manipulate us.

See, our ego has the persuasive ability to create illusions that *feel real* only within our subconscious mind (where it makes all the rules). *And since we human beings have yet to discover the sacred truth that defines us we are constantly being 'man-handled' by our man-made minds.*

Okay, based upon the above statement, allow me to ask you a critical question. How much of your subconscious mind do you control?

Chapter X

Although the real life question is, how much of 'you' does your subconscious mind control?

See, as we human beings seek our true purpose in life we tend to use familiar human images to help us interpret our way. Humanity is conditioned to rely on the notion that our human framework is what is used to gage and construct the foundation of our reality.

Therefore, we survey our respective societies and then draft our life's mission based upon familiar human images. And once we select our comparable ensemble, we proceed to use this architecture as the true blueprint to structure our purpose in life. Hence, we are conditioned to believe that our *physical images* are the determining symbols, which define our capabilities and our true meaning in life.

Thus, we are all confined to our own *inappropriate* bogus boxes. And each *man-made box* has been labeled and color coded as follows: *White Box, Black Box, Brown Box, Yellow Box, etc.* And this concealed state of subconscious living is suffocating the life out of us.

With all this said, please know *who we think we are* constructs our limiting beliefs. However, realizing the essence of who we are, will release us from our man-made caskets. And upon encountering this level of knowing, this comprehension will disable our limiting beliefs. Once our subconscious mind is formerly introduced to the *sole/soul* truth we will know that only the sky is our limit.

Humanity must try to understand that what we have deemed to be true about our *'selves'* is only based upon our man-made beliefs. And if we genuinely want to experience the truth, then we must *think* far beyond what our mind will allow us to perceive.

Do you ever wonder why we human beings are so greedy and insatiable? Do you ever think to your 'self', why we never seem

to be satisfied with what we have and why we are always driven to obtain more?

We human beings will never be satisfied with what we *materially* possess. Considering, what we materially acquire has no true value or substance; therefore we will always yearn for more. But the ultimate question is, if we are always driven to obtain more, then how will we ever be *fulfilled*?

This is why our ego creates a selfish craving for more and commits us to an extreme devotion of want. Some people's ego tends to make them envious of something that they have never desired before—only because it's another man's possession.

Whether we human beings are aware of this or not, our ego is taking us on a reckless *mind trip* towards failure and *self-destruction*, and this careless journey contradicts our real reason for *Being,* which is to obtain *fulfillment* and *joy* through *existing life.*

However, traveling through life with our ego will never harbor true satisfaction and delight because our ego has an *insatiable* appetite. And the reality is, in most cases the material items that we sacrifice our lives for are not so much for our own personal satisfaction but to make an *envious impression* upon others.

Our ego makes us seek what it temporarily wants by keeping us occupied and exhausted through tracking down short lived happiness. And once our euphoria dissipates, *then it's back to the track.* We human beings must discern, due to our ego's ravenous appetite, no matter what we *'materially'* feed it—it will always hunger for more.

I'm sure it's no secret that the more power we human beings possess, the more power we want. And the *selfish* power we seize goes straight to our subconscious mind or in other words, goes straight to our *heads.* Hence the expression, "*His Ego has given him a Big Head!*"

Chapter X

Due to the uncontrolled attention that we relinquish to our subconscious mind our man-made paradigm has in turn been able to convince us that our human image is what really defines us.

Well, please allow me this moment to outline in detail why we are under the impression that our physical framework represents who we are.

What's astonishing is how our beliefs have convinced us that our true nature *lies* within our *physical attributes*. It's as if our *material makeup* really defines our *intangible awareness*. We must try to understand that the beliefs that we have been dealt, for countless years, have been playing *poker* with humanity. And our subconscious mind, based upon the man-made concepts that it has been programmed to manage, will always be obsessed with ensuring that we perceive our human images as the *trump card* in this man-made game that we call life.

<u>Now allow me to explain how our mind is able to wield us into thinking that our physical framework represents our true nature</u>:

Please understand that our mind has been hard at work escorting us towards worshipping our human images in such a way, that we have categorically separated our *'selves'* from one another. And through this division, which is contingent upon our physical reflection, we have all collectively developed *individual cultures, belief systems, and behavioral patterns* which all simulate the following human images that we have been conditioned to represent: *Black, White, Hispanic, Asian, etc.*

Now as we human beings mature, our *racial* characteristics and our *cultural behaviors,* which we *believe* are associated with our specific *self-images* are now ingrained and then recycled and bestowed upon generation after generation, which in turn makes it appear as if our human attributes and behavior are simply a part of our *physical nature*. This is where the real problem *lies*; our *recycled man-made convictions* are a form of *mental abuse*.

<u>*Here is what I mean*</u>:

Although there may be some constructive characteristics laced within our paradigms, there's a boatload of destructive information that we incoherently live by. This means we unknowingly feed our *'selves'* with pain and suffering and then proceed to *regurgitate* these detrimental issues upon our children. This upchuck immobilizes our children and hinders them from having a beautiful and loving life experience.

Parents please know this is the worst case of child abuse that is currently **'unknown'** *to humankind.*

We human beings must make a valid effort to try and comprehend that there is nothing physical about our true nature. However, since we exist under the man-made notion that our human forms represent us, this *automatically* translates into a man-made belief that our true nature can only be physically defined. Humanity must ultimately discern that only the *sol/soul* exemplifies our natural nature.

Even our health issues that appear to be *physically genetic* all stem from our *man-made cultures.* Hence, the foods that we eat are directly connected to our cultures; which in turn defines our *physical ailments.* And since we view a human being's culture as being predominantly associated with one's **physical** image; **Physicians** traditionally diagnose our *physical health* problems as being **physically** genetic.

With all this being said, please grasp our genuine nature does not correlate with our physical attributes. Our man-made issues are a byproduct of a *self-image program* that we all *incoherently* act upon.

Do you realize because we are unaware of our divine potential we fail to tap into the glorious possibilities that are tucked away within our subconscious minds? And due to this absence of knowing, these beliefs actually limit our divine power.

Chapter X

Hence, we human beings lack the power of love because we have in turn relinquished our free will to our man-made beliefs. Therefore, instead of us being able to 'Will' what we desire out of life, our man-made egos 'Will' what they 'selfishly' want.

<u>Let me ask you a question. What does free your mind mean?</u>

Well, the way it appears today, our mind is already emancipated. And it seems as if our mind has predominantly freed it *'self'* and is now liberated to do whatever it wills.

Humanity must try to acknowledge that we are suffering from mental slavery and our egos are our masters. Thus, we must acknowledge by being in *sole/soul* control of our thoughts and awareness, this action alone, in accordance with Universal law, will force our egos to relinquish our universal gift of free will. This in turn, will free us from our minds' plantation.

Thus, this is when we will shout and quote Dr. Martin Luther King Jr. and say, *"Free at last, free at last. Thank God Almighty, we are free at last."*

Therefore, if you do decide to free your mind, please make sure that you are freeing your man-made identity from your subconscious mind

Hence, as Jesus said, or man's interpretation of what Jesus may have meant; "Your mind must be cleared of the falsehoods of this realm if you are to be taught Eternal Truth."

Translation: Your subconscious mind must be free of your *man-made perception of self* and your *man-made interpretation of life*, in order for you to discover that *you* are the *Eternal Truth* which resides within your human form.

<u>Now allow me to ask you, What is Free Will?</u>

Free will means having the freedom to do what we *Will* with our subconscious mind. However, our *Will* can only be exhibited if we maintain 'conscious' control of our mind. Nonetheless, the *Will Power* humanity was blessed with now belongs to our egos and our egos now *will* what they want upon us.

By Universal law our subconscious mind was assigned to be our *Guardian Angel* to *protect* and *serve* us. Thus, until we awaken to our *universal presence,* our egos will continue to *police* us by keeping our thoughts *locked up and confined to irrelevant time* (commonly referred to as *the past and the future).*

<u>Well speaking of time, do you think that it is time that you demand your **Will** back</u>?

Do you know what I have discovered to be extremely sad? Humanity hasn't even died yet; however we have already signed over our *Wills* to our egos. We human beings have surrendered our *Will* to our mind and beyond our knowledge we have all become *willing servants* to our man-made beliefs.

Our lack of Will Power is the primary reason why we human beings only partially exist in the real world; hence this is the real reason why we seldom get the most out of life.

Although most of humanity lives a subconscious life, we must realize that we are not deceased yet. Therefore, we need to inform our mind that we want our Will back! Only through this vital acquisition *will* we ever be able to successfully gain freedom from our minds and end our human suffering.

Do you believe we human beings live an unconscious life?

It seems that most Spiritual Teachers believe we human beings live *unconscious lives*. In my opinion, we really do not suffer from a state of *unconsciousness,* but more from a *state of 'Being' unaware.* Thus, we human beings are *unaware* of the fact that we robotically live our lives according to the man-made concepts that we believe define who we are.

Chapter X

See, what is crucial to our current existence, as well as to our future survival, is we must realize if we never gain full control of our awareness then we will never gain dominion of our lives.

Please understand our devilish behavior is not a product of our divine nature. Our disorderly conduct is a byproduct of our diabolical conditioning that has distorted our perception of *self* and *life*. Thus, it is only our *man-made conditioning* that makes us function and see our *'selves'* and life the way we do.

Do you recognize enlightenment does not exist within the current parameters of our subconscious minds?

We human beings will never discover genuine enlightenment within the current parameters of our subconscious minds as long as our *thoughts and awareness* are in the *constant motion* of *picturing dreary images* that are religiously being re-played by our minds. In order for our subconscious minds to be enlightened we must become aware that we are the *soulful light* that shines within the human form.

In summary, it will be next to impossible to find that *eternal light* switch that will allow us to plug into who we are as long as we continue to aimlessly fumble around in the darkness and man-made clutter that presently occupies the attic of our subconscious minds.

As we conclude this chapter, I have one final question for you: Do you want to know how we can refurbish our minds and reconstruct our egos?

I believe Dr. Wayne Dyer refers to the word EGO as being an acronym for *"Edging God Out."* Well, I am going to modify the meaning of this acronym a tad and I am going to say that our E.G.O. stands for "**Exit** God Out."

Now here is how we begin to remodel our minds to eventually model the true nature of this Universe.

The Man-Made Mind

When we as souls recognize our place in the realm of true reality as conscious human Beings, we will commence to move back into our initial place of residence, which is the human heart. And once we move back into our *humble* abode the lines of communication with this Universe will open wide.

Once our communication channels are accessible to the loving energy of this Universe the renovations will begin by replacing the waste that currently fills our minds, with divine attributes such as: *Love, Honor, Respect, Kindness, Gratitude, etc.*

Now, after these gratifying traits have taken hold of our minds they will proceed to replace the current filth of: *Fear, Hate, Dishonesty, Greed, Selfishness, etc.,* which to me, is the true definition of: *"A mind is a terrible thing to waste!"*

And once our minds have been revamped with loving characteristics we will witness the renewal of the genuine essence of this Universe entering into our lives.

How you may ask?

Well, because Good *(God)* and Evil (D*evil*) cannot share the same space, and once the true essence of this Universe moves into our subconscious mind, our EGO has no choice but to *Exit* the premises.

See the 'E' that represents the word *Exit* justly vanishes; which now leaves us with the two letters G and O. Now *'GO'* simply means it is time for our EGO to do just that—GO!

So, with the eviction of our EGO, in comes a new occupant. And since our EGO is now *done,* the 'D' from the word **DONE** now forms into the last position of the two letters that are still remaining, which are G.O. So, it appears that G.O.D. is now occupying our subconscious minds.

But hold on; we are not done yet!

Chapter X

Despite what we have been conditioned to believe, there is only *a Sol/Sole energy that defines this Universe*. Therefore, the final three letters remaining from the word *D<u>ONE</u>* will be placed in front of the word G.O.D. So now, who do we have residing within our subconscious mind as a new loving tenant?

That's right **ONE GOD!**

Now, once our subconscious mind has been groomed and landscaped with the loving essence of *'One God'* or in better words; with 'One Loving' idea of this Universe, even an incoherent or a *subconscious* thought will make us feel glorious. Hence, we as children of this divine Universe must cease listening to our minds and stop believing that we are hopeless. *Thus, in the absence of man-made beliefs, we inherent everything!*

XI

The Human Avatar

Do you know that our 'physical' form is our Human Avatar?

Yeah I know; I am sure your immediate response to this statement is huh?

<u>*Well before you skip this chapter (or worse, close this book), please allow me to explain*</u>:

The insinuation that the physical form is our Human Avatar is *not* based upon the idea that I believe that we are blue Beings from another planet. However, what I am implying is that what we see in the mirror is a *physical* reflection of our *Human Machine*. Meaning, the physical form that we have been conditioned to believe as being us is, in reality, a perfectly designed *out of this world outfit* that has been tailored made to suit the *spiritual energy* of who we really are.

In other words, what I am trying to convey is our *external image* does not bear our *internal truth*. Although our external image does not represent who we truly are, please know that I am not saying that our human forms are irrelevant. What I am simply stating is that our human forms are only suited to dress our divine nature.

In further words, if we proceed to think that the human shell defines us, then we will continue to reconfirm our religious convictions by believing that we are not divine and one with the nature of this Universe. See, our mortal image is not a true reflection of this Universe, considering the *immortal* **Sun/Sol** *of this Universe*

Chapter XI

is what characterizes the divine energy of this Universe—and us as human beings as well.

Okay, our journey has reached a pivotal point; so I ask you, do you still believe what you see in the mirror is the real you? In other words, do you still believe that the racial labels that have been assigned to us by society, genuinely defines who we are?

Well if you still vaguely believe in this misconceived concept, do you realize the racial tags that have been applied to our physical forms have been embedded into our sub-conscious mind in order to separate us from other human beings?

Well, if you have answered yes, in regards to still believing in the concept that it is only your *man-made race* that defines you, then please know what you see in the mirror is theoretically an *Alien!* Considering, if you still believe that your physical image is indeed you, then this means the *true you* has been completely **alien**ated from your reality.

In further words, please know that our reflection in the mirror will always *lie to us,* because it is incapable of reflecting the *true essence* of who we are, beyond what we physically see. Thus, our reflection in the mirror is nothing more than a *man-made concept* that we have been conditioned to believe is us.

<u>Now, allow me to explain how my reference to our physical form being our Human Avatar, correlates with the motion picture Avatar:</u>

Avatar is a relatively old movie that was released back in 2009. However, if you haven't seen this movie, I suggest that you watch it with a lucid heart and a *wide open* sub-conscious mind in order to capture the real essence of the movie.

Avatar's main character, *Jake,* is a disabled former-marine who finds himself thrust into a hostile environment on an alien planet filled with exotic life forms, including humanoids called the Navi.

The Human Avatar

Jake's mind or more so the ***'soul' of Jake*** is to be transferred into the body of a synthetically grown Navi to aid in learning their ways and convincing them to vacate their ancestral homes so the Earthlings (a heavily armed mining company) can operate there.

Now, while the soul of Jake is within the Navi avatar's body he finds himself torn between two worlds; the Spiritual world of the Navi and the Egoist world of Mankind.

The Navi were a people of peace and discipline who lived in harmony with all forms of nature; whereas the Human world was a world of high technology and disregard for nature (including the Navi). In particular the mining company wanted the Navi to relocate from their ancestral home so they could mine there.

The movie Avatar exemplifies how the <u>soul</u> within any type of life form is all that defines our true nature.

In the end Jake falls in love with Neytiri (the chief's daughter) and helps the Navi fight the mining company's mini army.

The movie includes a customary greeting among the Navi "I see you." It is explained to Jake that this phrase is more profound than the English translation, having the meaning that I see the soul of who you are (the internal, cognitive Being) beyond your physical form.

This says it all!

See, when we are able to live coherently through the human heart we become more capable of seeing beyond what is irrelevant. In the grand scheme of our reality, it really doesn't matter the shape of one's shell; all that really matters is the nature of one's soul.

Okay, here is a nice hypothetical example for you.

Let's say we Earthlings eventually have a successful mission to Mars and we encounter what we call Martians. Do you know what these Martians would probably say to us Earthlings upon our arrival if they did not possess a Martian Ego?

<u>*Welcome my 'Sol' siblings!*</u>

See, these Martians would most likely be *neighboring sols/souls* within this Universe, experiencing life on planet Mars, in the physical form of Martians.

Whether we discern this or not, our **Solar** System is one massive system of *Almighty Consciousness;* and considering Mars is our neighboring Solar Planet these Martians would receive the same *solar energy* that we do, except in a different strength. Hence, even this would apply to *"love thy neighbor."*

As a resident conscious Being of this place we call Earth, the human form was designed to be our personal avatar, which is a *highly advanced physical system used to house our **solar** energy.* And although some of us share similar models, each Human Avatar is uniquely designed from head to toe.

See, the human anatomy is a divinely designed machine which is controlled by the central nervous system. Every function, reaction, response, perspective, and feeling is *physically processed* via this glorious systematic enterprise.

The human nervous system is comprised of the *influential* mainframe *(the brain or the subconscious mind)* and the human control panel, which is called the spinal cord. Thus, every aspect of our *Human Avatar's* behavior and our *Human Avatar's* interaction is conducted through this human circuitry.

Therefore, since our brain or subconscious mind is the vital master to our Human Avatar's *expression,* this should behoove humanity to ensure that our subconscious mind receives initial direction from a loving source of *divine intercommunication.* Hence, the *sol energy* of who we are is indeed the *true passion* beyond the human flesh of our personal avatar.

See, what I am clearly trying to convey is there is no part of *our* physical anatomy that defines who we are. This reference also pertains to *our* physical brain.

In reality, *our* physical framework is not responsible for *our* unique personality, *our* untouchable consciousness, or *our* intangible thoughts. And please acknowledge, as *Solar Beings of this Universe,* our physical framework *solely/souly* belongs to us and not vice versa. Which means *we,* as *conscious souls of this Universe,* do not belong to our physical form.

Please allow me to ask you a question, do you recognize when we make certain statements such as, 'I' left 'my soul' on the field or 'I' poured 'my soul' out in this book, we are unknowingly insinuating that our 'physical form' holds priority over 'us', which is the conscious soul. This means, we are proclaiming that our 'human flesh' is what truly defines us.

In other words, we human beings must try to learn and discern how to reverse our *form* of thinking and come to the sound *conscious conclusion* that we don't have a soul; however as being a soul reflection of this Universe, we indeed have a human form. Hence, it is only the conscious energy of *us,* the souls, which brings *who we physically think we are* to life.

See, we write our life's destiny via our thoughts and awareness. Thus, we are the *programmers* that create the *program* that is encoded within our mainframe. And once our thoughts are uploaded and **'saved'** into our subconscious mind; our subconscious mind, being the *obedient comrade* that it is, will always *honor the code* that has been *thoughtfully* written.

Now allow me to ask you an even 'deeper' question; are '<u>YOU</u>' comfortable in your own skin? In other words, are '<u>YOU</u>' comfortable in the 'skin' you are in? The under-<u>lying</u> truth is most of us are not!

Chapter XI

I am sure most of us are only familiar with this expression on a *subconscious level.* Therefore, have you ever taking the time to *consciously* explore and examine this expression to determine if **'I'** am in my 'skin'—*then who am 'I'?*

Although, I do not subscribe to the religious notion of being a born sinner, believing however that *you* are defined by the skin is by far the most *'selfish'* sin.

See, honoring the idea that your skin or *flesh* defines you, subconsciously creates an ***everlasting*** relationship with your 'self.' Through this *self-belief* you become *self*-conscious, *self*-serving, and *self*-made, because you begin to subconsciously or automatically live your life in accordance to the man-made concepts that have been assigned to the 'skin' you are in. Whether, you realize this or not, believing subconsciously that you are a **'physical'** Being is what enslaves you, devours your power, and robs you of your sacred energy. Why you might ask? *Well, because in your true essence, there is absolutely nothing physical about you!*

As a religious believer you may be hell-bent on believing that *someone else* is going to eventually save you from your 'self'; however in reality this task is totally your responsibility.

Once you 'awaken' to *truly know* that 'I' am the **unseen** conscious observer or *"The Soul"* within my skin, only then will the self-made shackles that have been constructed to imprison you begin to dissolve and you will experience an *electrifying feeling of truth* that will set you free forever.

The 'Sol' of who we are and our Human Avatar was designed to perform and function as follows.

The **sol**ar energy from the Sun provides our Human Avatar with its life source of fuel and energy through the spiritual air the human body breathes. Upon consuming this spiritual air, our human heart then distributes the conscious energy of this

Universe throughout the human form to substantiate our physical existence.

Our subconscious mind is then assigned the responsibility of *automatically controlling* the physical mechanics of our bodily functions, along with providing the designated soul with a loving and enjoyable physical experience, which is solely contingent upon the soul's awareness of authentic life.

Hence, when we are consciously in tune with the existing moment, this allows our subconscious mind to be a wide open recipient towards receiving *enlightenment* from this Universe. Thus, as children of the sacred Sun/Sol, we can now begin our spiritual mission towards co-creating a virtuous loving world as prosperous human beings.

Now, I know this chapter may have been a bit *out of this world* for some individuals. However, beyond all the alien theories, I hope everyone *sensed* the primary point centered on this chapter. And that is what truly defines us goes far beyond what we physically see. In other words, *there is far more to us than meets the physical eye.*

XII

Believing Versus Knowing

What I find interesting is that we human beings only *believe* in *a 'fearful' man-made idea of this Universe*; but the real question is do we really *know* the divine nature of this Universe? We also say that we *believe* in love; but the true inquiry is do we truly *know* what defines divinity?

No matter what we say we *believe* in, there will always be a degree of uncertainty that is associated with our beliefs. However, tapping into the nature of *knowing* is always complimented with *real* reassurance.

Therefore, with the above being stated, do you really think if our entire lives are based upon man-made beliefs, there could actually be a difference between believing versus knowing?

<u>Well here is my opinion</u>:

The primary difference between believing versus knowing is, *beliefs* are constructed by *man-made concepts* and *knowing* is a *bona fide feeling* inspired by something far more divine.

Our paradigms are comprised of countless years of suspicious man-made data that has been deliberately manufactured and produced to govern our thoughts, which in turn has constructed a faulty foundation for what we believe.

In other words, if our intuition does not provide us with a sound sense of perception, then a thought formulated from our man-made paradigm is nothing more than the following: *I hope for my sake what I believe is actually true.* This uncertainty is generated because the dubious information that has been dumped into our subconscious mind, for the most part, has not been *consciously challenged*.

To expand upon this even further, every man-made belief recorded by our subconscious mind is a conditioned conviction which has convinced us that our beliefs are indeed the Gospel. Pure insight and enlightenment can only be articulated by an energy that is divine and then whispered into our subconscious mind. This is why when you find your *'self'* in a situation and *you* don't know what to do, you are often told to listen to your heart. Because this is where the *sole/soul* truth *initially* lives.

The universal essence of who we are will not *lie* to us. However, what appears to be a constant habit *is how our man-made sense of self seems to lie to us religiously.*

<u>Please try to comprehend the pertinence of the following statement</u>:

If your beliefs contain a fraction of suspicion then this minuscule amount of doubt means that you should seek to cast certain beliefs out.

Okay, I am sure that it is safe to say that typically a thought is formed first, then some sort of 'feeling' soon follows based upon the result of our thinking.

Now, allow me to ask you a very interesting question; have you ever experienced the opposite? Meaning, first you received a divine feeling which then created a glorious thought?

In most cases we don't experience a divine feeling first since we are way too busy listening to what our ego has to say. See, our thoughts and our awareness are frequently focused upon what we have been *previously conditioned to believe,* which leaves us with no time to hear what our Universe *presently* has to say.

The main reason we human beings struggle with encountering the sacred truth is because we are addicted to the man-made concepts that we have been taught to believe. Until we figure out how to properly operate our thoughts and our awareness we will never possess control of our lives.

See, the moment we learn how to ignore certain thoughts that have been constructed by man, this action will then silence the annoying noise maker—our ego. And once we are no longer faced with distracting man-made beliefs we will then be available to really listen to what our Universe has to convey. When we are free of being fixated on disturbing and destructive beliefs, this will be the definition of having a true *peace of mind.*

See when our awareness is *still*; our subconscious mind is at peace and it can now *quietly sense* what our Universe is attempting to transmit. And once we sense a glorious feeling of certainty and this sensation is bestowed upon our subconscious mind *then we behold the Universe's true nature of divine wisdom!*

This is how we bond and build a loving relationship with our Universe, as well as, with all forms of life. Unfortunately, this is an extreme challenge considering we do not function under a controlled state of consciousness.

However, during this *moment of silence*, please know that you are not spending time with your *'self'*, this is a special moment spent simply bonding with the nature of one's *Being.* And as a human Being, the divine nature of one's Being is born before our human form. The sacred energy of *the soul,* which is who we are, is *present* before the man-made image of who we think we are begins to conceal us.

Chapter XII

Do you believe we are less knowledgeable than we think?

See, our man-made intelligence makes us believe that we know so much. However, the uncertainty of not knowing who we really are does not produce knowledge, it only forms beliefs.

When we encounter a feeling of intuition that is laced with the truth, this profound feeling creates a true sense of knowing. However, this divine sense of knowing cannot be taught; it can only be detected through a sacred sense of **Ah Ha!**

See, we were all born into this world *knowing nothing*. And if our man-made IQ makes us believe that we now know everything, then please know one thing, until we discover our true identity, we will unfortunately die as we were born—still *knowing nothing!*

Hence, our *man-made Intelligence Quotient* is only capable of furnishing us with a shallow sense of who we *think* we are; whereas our *Universal Spiritual Quotient* will always provide us with a deeper sense of *knowing* who we are.

As a whole we have all been schooled by our egos and we have all graduated with *dishonor;* considering we have *failed* to uncover who we really are, as well as, determine how to consciously live and love, as divine human beings.

Do you discern discovering the truth is humanity's grandest challenge; considering our "lying beliefs" refuse to get out of our way?

I know humanity may find it difficult to conceptualize that we are more infinite than our human image. Since our lives have been a vigorous process of distorted self-conditioning; which has been geared towards fixating our subconscious minds on our human form as being our authentic self and through this inaccurate perception of *being only human* we are left to struggle with not *Being enough.*

I understand the complexity of imagining that we are far more than cells, organs, muscles, and tissue. I honor the fact that it may be challenging to comprehend that there is a greater substance that lives beyond what we physically see—considering our beliefs have convinced us otherwise. However, please perceive our subconscious mind by Universal Law cannot successfully function without our controlled conscious awareness.

This mental disconnection of subconscious mind, minus us, *the loving soul,* is what's creating our failures and frustrations in life. Therefore, until we gain full control of our consciousness we will continue to operate throughout life labeled as *out of order* and *out of control.*

So with all this said, I do realize why our awareness is so connected to our human forms and yet so *'informal'* to whom we really are.

Do you know the truth is not something to believe?

For those who believe in God, please believe in this; the real essence of this Universe does not want us to believe in anything. This loving source of power simply wants us to *know one thing,* and that is *who we really are!* Hence, the last thing this Universe wants for us is to be bulldozed into believing in man-made concepts that conflicts with our divine nature.

Please know being coerced into believing what is supposedly true is *unnatural.* No one should have to be reminded *religiously* as to what the alleged truth is. Considering once we unveil our true nature, then the truth will *naturally* prevail through us.

<u>And with this being said, please allow me to provide you with my perception of the truth</u>.

There is no soul who is born of this world that *arrived* here *believing* in man's version of this Universe. Thus, there is no human being who was born <u>*naturally knowing*</u> that this Universe is a Supernatural Man that judges our motives and will severely punish those who do not accept 'Him' or 'His' wishes. We only accept this *irrational* story as being true because we have been *force fed to have faith* in its validity.

So, here is some divine food for thought. Any man-made story that projects the idea of being <u>unbelievable</u> should leave a bad taste in your mouth and should be considered distasteful or untrustworthy. Therefore, any information that is not *sensible* should not be stomached or believed.

Furthermore, if you are someone who is sincerely seeking the truth, then you must first comprehend that the truth you seek is *not visible*. In other words, the truth that we seek is bestowed upon our human form as a *powerful electromagnetic 'feeling'* and <u>not</u> in the form of a vision.

Thus, as I mentioned in a prior chapter, *how we feel* creates the foundation to our reality. *And once you encounter the truth, it is a feeling like no other*. Hence, the truth is a feeling that you do not question, because the truth is accompanied by feelings of *certainty, peace, love, and joy*. And what's interesting is we human beings occasionally experience a fleeting feeling that warrants the truth; however, we unfortunately fail to realize that this amazing congruent feeling is the energy that defines us.

<u>Here is what I mean</u>:

As it relates to some Christians, during certain services, their Pastor, Priest, Preacher, or Reverend may deliver an *electrifying* sermon that completely resonates with the soul of who they are. Hence, they will immediately encounter a strong electromagnetic feeling that is so overwhelming that they immediately believe that this *electrical current* that is flowing throughout their entire body is indeed the spirit of Jesus. Hence, this is what some Christians refer to as the *"Holy Ghost."*

The irony is this feeling that *you* come in contact with is actually <u>the soul of who you are briefly plugging into the electrifying energy of your own divine nature</u>. However, because we are oblivious to our true nature the Christian God that man calls Jesus is rewarded with all the glory.

Do you know what the irony is between 'believing' versus 'knowing'?

Well, until you *personally experience* what I proclaim to know, in terms of what truly defines us, then what I speak of is going to appear only as my man-made belief.

Now if you have allowed the words within this book to soak into your heart and into your subconscious mind and you have arrived at this passage, there may be a small or even large spark of interest that may have created an *inspiring sensation* which makes <u>*you feel*</u> that what is written within this narrative could actually be the bona fide truth.

However, for some of you, if you choose to refer to the current state of your subconscious mind for validation, your man-made paradigm will most likely try to persuade you into believing otherwise by sending you warning signals which may read as follows: *What he speaks of are only his beliefs; therefore you need to maintain your own!*

And as I just mentioned above, until *you* personally experience the truth for your *'self'*, what I say will always appear only as my personal belief. Hence, if *you* never encounter what I speak of, then please do as your *'self'* instructs and *don't believe a word that I say.*

Adopting another formed belief will not produce the degree of knowing that will be able to introduce you to the divine essence of who you are. In other words, *simply believing that this information is true will not be enough to reveal the real you.* So once again, considering that you have not fathomed what I have

Chapter XII

encountered, my sense of knowing will only bear the resemblance of another man-made belief.

Thus, I know in the absence of knowing, a man-made belief is what every human being believes in. However, we will never be able to envision the truth if man's beliefs continue to 'lie' in our way.

Therefore, if this were merely my belief, then trust me, you would not be reading this book. Considering, in the absence of *true knowing*, I would not possess the divine **know**how to create such a book.

Here is a prime example of what I mean, as it relates to a distinct 'feeling' between believing and knowing.

Okay, let's say you are an individual who has yet to have a child of your own. But you have several close friends frequently sharing with you what a joy it is to have children and how they bring true meaning to your life.

Well, you may sincerely *believe* that this information is indeed accurate. However, until you encounter this beautiful experience personally, it is impossible for you to obtain a true sense of *knowing* what an *incredible feeling* it really is to have a child of your own. In other words, no one can *make you believe* what it *feels* like to be a parent since this *degree of knowing* can only be *personally experienced.*

Every word written within *Lying Beliefs* was not constructed to gain beliefs. I am more driven to try and drive our awareness towards the *sole/soul* essence of whom we are; which is a *miraculous energy of conscious life* that lives beyond what we have been conditioned to believe.

I know I can't personally rescue anyone. This job is *solely/souly* your obligation. However, I can attempt to construct a *sensible* platform by way of compiling enough *rational* information that we may already be privy to, in hopes that it will create an *enlightening spark* that will *light* the way to discover the divine energy of who we are.

See, what I speak of goes far beyond any man-made concept. You may never comprehend what I mean until *you* discover this divine sense of knowing for your '*self*'.

Once again, this level of knowing is not a life lesson that can be taught, it can only be *uncovered*. However, the *life lessons* that we human beings are often *taught* essentially *lessen our lives*. As long as we continue to hand over our divine power to our beliefs we human beings will remain *un-wholly.*

Whenever we relinquish the soul of who we are to a Questionable man-made belief, this action severs our relationship with divinity, which will forever leave us as *un-divine human beings!*

Thus, here is the colossal difference between believing and knowing:

<u>Beliefs breed fear, hatred, and intolerance. Knowing unleashes our divine nature, which is the Power of Love. Hence "Knowledge is Power!"</u>

XIII

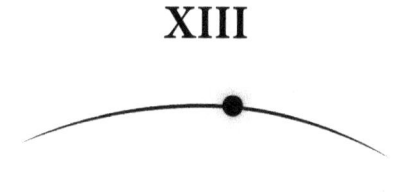

In the End

To my fellow human beings:

I want to thank you for granting *Lying Beliefs* your attention. And I hope *'In The End'* we human beings as a *whole* will eventually awaken to our universal nature. Hence, I hope this book assisted you in some way with the rebirth of who you truly are.

In other words, I hope you found the wisdom shared in this document as an *enlightening experience* which was able to shine a *soulful light* upon a brand new you.

Question: as you come to the conclusion of this book, do you still believe that it will take a miracle to shed your 'self' in order to suit you? In other words, do you still think that we need to discover a solution to this egoist virus?

Okay, let's say that we developed a cure to obliterate this selfish man-made ailment and the antidote was downloaded to our mainframe. Well, in order to create an elixir to remedy this man-made program, it is going to take a **miracle**.

<u>However, guess what? I have great news</u>!

See, once we as divine souls evolve and become *whole* with our genuine nature we will naturally become that *miracle solution* that is capable of curing our man-made suffering. Considering, in our true essence, *we are all the <u>Miracle of Life</u>!*

Chapter XIII

If this literary portrait has been vividly sketched, whereas so it was able to reveal its divine purpose by inspiring a movement or a shift in your awareness towards a more sacred sense of knowing, then I have fulfilled my mission.

Please know by living as *divine human beings* we contain the phenomenal ability to make a global change and rectify our man-made suffering. We can rid ourselves of this egoist virus if we all decide to tap into our universal given gift of *free will*. And upon tapping into our free will, we will then possess the ability to expand the chambers of our hearts and allow this Universe to provide us with a Celestial Anti-Virus which in turn will destroy, or at least diminish, this egoist disease.

Now, once this egotistical cancer is eliminated, we, as a *soul product* of this Universe, can then proceed to install a divine Anti-Virus software to prevent our egos from returning. And once this Anti-Virus software is operational, we can then begin to move forward with re-programming our subconscious minds by way of installing software that more accurately defines who we are— which would be appropriately labeled as *Glorious Thoughts!*

Thus, this amended version of our subconscious mind will be tailor made to properly suit a more prosperous human **Being** such as:

Being more conscious

Being more blissful

Being more loyal

Being more joyful

Being more peaceful

And last but not least, 'Being' more Divine!

Hence, I think you get the portrait. The real picture here is to place *Being* in front of everything, *except for 'Being' only human.*

Please note, the only way we will ever be showered with these glorious feelings is by way of *Being whole* with this Universe, *Being whole* with our Planet, and of course *Being whole* with each other.

The natural transformation of becoming a *Wholly* human being will only take place once the transmission of these loving expressions take hold of our subconscious minds.

Now, once these divine emotions have been embraced by our subconscious minds, we as the *Being,* will start to lovingly manifest ourselves throughout our human forms as we were destined to since the beginning of our existence.

Hey, do you remember when the late great John Lennon sang "Imagine"?

Well *imagine* on a *sacred sunny day* we awaken to a <u>Whole</u> New World where our primary focus is no longer about just being egotistical humans, but on *Being* loving human beings.

Imagine if our man-made *garbage*, which was holding us back as well as weighing us down, was *trashed* upon the completion of our soulful discovery.

Now *imagine* we are free of all excessive man-made baggage and we are now transporting a light carry-on container filled with nothing more than our *universal possession,* which is now an updated and newly reformatted subconscious mind.

Imagine upon our arrival to a better understanding we all adhered to the same mission statement.

Imagine we all possessed the same code of conduct as well as the same code of ethics.

Imagine we all genuinely loved one another, considering we know that we all shared the same common **'Sol'** and we were all striving to achieve the same common goal.

Chapter XIII

Imagine if we had everything that we needed in abundance and therefore we wanted for nothing.

Through behaving less like egotistical humans and more like *'Wholly'* human beings our *imaginations* can become our *reality!*

If our new and improved subconscious minds *automatically* made us exude the divine essence of this Universe there would be no further room for any man-made rhetoric to affect our psyche in regards to our former *self*.

Okay, with this being said, I guess we have said farewell to our past, so does this now mean we need to 'worry' about our future?

See, there is a big difference between worrying about our future and envisioning our future. Hence, it's a beautiful thing to envision our future; however we should not live there, until we get there.

Worry is a terrible waste of our imagination because worry creates nothing but it can destroy everything. It is a source of *fear, anxiety, and depression*. And these *man-made emotions* are the key ingredients that form the most negative impact on our lives, our society, and our world.

The irony is, once we make the conversion into loving human beings, we will fix our problems of the past and this resolution will in turn resolve our future problems of tomorrow. Thus, as divine human beings, we possess no worry since our attention no longer *dwells* upon the future. Considering, outside of the present moment, genuine life has yet to exist.

Therefore, with the non-existence of worry there will always be a *brighter tomorrow* and a *Happily Ever After.*

Let me ask you a question: do you know what time it is?

In the End

Well, it's time to say "farewell" to yesterday and "hello" to today. Don't live worrying about tomorrow since tomorrow has yet to become the *present*.

Understand that *Being* present is impossible, especially when our presence is constantly being blanketed by our past problems. We need to resist reliving our *past failures* in our present moment since the gift of life that was previously granted cannot be rewrapped.

Therefore, start relishing in the right here and right now and enjoy the *Gift of Life* which is a loving *present* that awaits our undivided attention each and every blessed moment. And please recognize, outside of *consciously appreciating* the immediate moment we are only *subconsciously worrying* about a moment that bears no relevance.

In conclusion, I feel as part of my life's calling the *'Spirit'* of this Universe has *inspired* me to deliver this message in hopes of rescuing those who are seeking the truth and wanting to reclaim their lives from their controlling egos. The purpose of this knowledge is to inspire us to reassess our current paradigms, which in turn will diminish some of our man-made convictions.

Lying Beliefs was written to heighten our awareness of authentic life which is forever *present*—but always ignored. This written depiction is constructed to facilitate and provide us with a formal introduction to our true genuine nature. And once we establish a solid bond with true reality we will then be promoted to an enlightening new life; not as humans, but as *Wholly* human beings.

Please be aware that we are all at war with our *'self'* assigned egos. Hence, we must comprehend that this battle with our ego is a fight to remove every *piece* of our *man-made* identity from our controlling mind. And if we are victorious, we will be blessed with a peaceful life, because we will have finally gained a peaceful subconscious mind.

However, we need to acknowledge that this battle cannot be won *selfishly*. We must rid ourselves of our selfish man-made principles which define our life's purpose as to only serve and help ourselves. In other words, victory can only manifest itself *through unity and total togetherness*.

Please recognize, we must not make an initial attempt to demolish our egos; we must first try to *diminish* them. We human beings must realize that this ego of ours is relentless. Therefore, we can't simply *fire* our ego and expect it not to retaliate; we must work to *manage* it out.

Thus, we must first give our ego a *verbal warning* by proclaiming: **_I AM_** now in charge of my life. And in most cases our verbal warning will need to be followed up with a *written warning* which would state: "*I* no longer need your services."

See, if every human being makes an initial effort to manage and control their self-assigned ego, then this will ultimately lead to the eradication of our egos. If we all slowly proceed to release our egos and migrate towards our true nature, which is love, then before we know it, we will have freed our '*selves*' of this self-destructive monster. And the only reason we are *afraid to let go* of our egos is because everyone else is *possessed* by one.

Please *"Let Go and Let God!" Or in other words, let go of your ego and let your Universal nature take over from here and now.*

As John Mayer says, *"We are all waiting on the World to Change." The irony is—we need to change!*

Hence, the World that rests within this divine Universe is perfect. It's the man-made world that exists within our subconscious minds that we *religiously* live by that really needs to change.

Even with this said please know as I mentioned in the beginning of this book, the information outlined in *Lying Beliefs* was not

In the End

created to make anyone believe that we should banish all man-made concepts and ideas.

There are numerous ideas and concepts that man has constructed that serve as a beautiful conscious experience. However, the sole/soul goal of this book is to *formally* introduce who we really are to our subconscious mind and try to have us discern that every man-made concept and idea only defines our conscious experience and should never be misconstrued to redefine us.

Thus, we human beings need to realize that we should never be defined by the information stored within our subconscious minds considering we are all born defined as '*Being*' divine.

So, please cease allowing man-made concepts to strip away your divinity. In other words, always stay true to the *real universal essence of you*.

May our divine Universe forever keep us inspired through spirit to do what is right, not only for ourselves, but also for our fellow human beings. And may the essence of love that originates within our hearts eventually find its way into our subconscious minds.

I hope this divine message was able to successfully speak to you—not loud and clear, but *profound and clear*. Trust in the truth that we are only divine as human beings, and please resist being *egotistically* coerced into *Being* only human. Furthermore, I hope *Lying Beliefs* serves as a *real solution* to what man has made us believe is a solution.

Okay, before I let you go, here is my final question: What does <u>unconditional love</u> mean to you?

Well, here is what it means to me. It means being able to love someone despite their *present condition* and being able to weather any storm with another human being *under any condition*.

However, in order to achieve *unconditional love*, we must first *un-condition* or *recondition* our subconscious mind to be able

Chapter XIII

to *automatically* display this level of love without us having to <u>*consciously*</u> *think* about it.

And now for my final words.

<u>*Please try to comprehend the reality of the following statement*</u>:

Every human being on this glorious planet, in their own way, suffers from what they *unknowingly* dwell upon within their subconscious minds. Thus, our egos live and survive *solely/souly* off of our *man-made* behavior.

Therefore, please know, as long as we live by the rules of our egos, our egos will always rule us. We human beings must come to realize that although there are rules to this Universe, this Universe is not ruled by any one image.

Thus, in regards to one's image, humanity must come to know that our man-made *'self'* is our *only* enemy. We human beings must understand that this glorious planet originated as Heaven on Earth. However, due to our <u>*lack of knowing*</u>, this Heavenly creation is slowly transforming into Hell on Earth.

We must awaken to bear witness that our beliefs are responsible for destroying this planet, as well as, all forms of life that inhabit it. We human beings must plunge deep into the soul of who we are, in order to sense that it is solely our <u>*self-serving*</u> man-made convictions that spawn our ever growing devilish societies. Hence, if we do not eventually *shift our awareness* to a better sense of knowing we will all perish by way of *'Self'* destruction!

Please know every Human Being on this sacred planet serves a divine purpose. However, it seems as if our world has convinced us that our primary purpose in life is to only serve our man-made beliefs. This has altered our divine reason for *"Being."*

We human beings must someday come to realize that our genuine nature is interconnected with this Universe. And it is only

In the End

the ill nature of our beliefs that not only disconnect us from one another; but also detach us from this divine Universe.

Therefore, we must cease defending the beliefs that man has made us believe are worth protecting. In other words, we should not be willing to defend and die for the man-made lies that lie deep within our subconscious minds or in the minds of others.

Hence, we human beings need to gain conscious control of our lives so that our *'Selves'* are no longer the *Rulers* of *'our'* thoughts and awareness!

<u>However, to conclude on a 'brighter' note, please consider the following statement</u>:

Even in the midst of our darkest day, regardless of what our ego may say, the divine love from our Universal **Sun** will forever shine our way.

One Love or *Sole/Soul Love* to All!

Personal Acknowledgments

Jose Paula

To my dear friend Jose Paula, I want to thank you very much for having the foresight, after a meeting you and I had, to introduce me to Joe Yazbeck. I am grateful that you pointed me in Joe's direction after hearing about my book. The reason why I am so appreciative is because my book, that I briefly spoke about, was not a bullet point that was associated with our meeting. Therefore, Jose, I am sincerely thankful my friend for your clairvoyance.

Joe Yazbeck

To Joe Yazbeck, whom I consider to be a true *Golden Spirit*. I want to thank you, my friend, for being the conductor, facilitator, and orchestrator surrounding the professional completion of my book.

I want to thank you for constantly keeping me on track and steering me in the right direction. Quite frankly, without your guidance and support *Lying Beliefs* would not have reached this level of professionalism. My sincerest thanks my friend.

Ginger Marks, Layout & Cover Designer

Dear Ginger I want to thank you for your candid feedback surrounding the initial production of my book. I want to thank you very much for helping me polish what was initially a rough draft of *Lying Beliefs*. Though most importantly, I want to thank you with all my heart for just *"wanting to help!"*

Philip Marks, Editor

Dear Philip, I want to thank you Sir very much for your diligence, your patience, and for your scientific expertise towards perfectly polishing my book. I was extremely fortunate to have a soul of your caliber and knowledge reviewing and editing my work. I am also grateful that you are someone who has a philosophical perspective that is in many ways similar to mine.

Words can barely express how appreciative I am for your time and dedication. Thank you Sir once again for a job well done!

Grasi Favoreto, Photographer

Dear Grasi, I want to say thank you very much for a well-done photo.

And last but not least, I have a *sole* acknowledgment; which I lovingly grant to this Universe for bestowing upon me the divine *knowhow* to create such a book.

INTERNET ACKNOWLEDGEMENTS

Chapter V: *Is Consciousness More Than Just A Mind?*
Conscious, Preconscious, and Unconscious: Freud's 3 Levels of Mind
psychology.about.com › ... › <u>Sigmund Freud</u> by Kendra Cherry

Chapter VI: *What Does God Mean To You?*
God - Wikipedia, the free encyclopedia
*en.wikipedia.org/wiki/**God***

Chapter VIII: *God's Immortal Soul (Sol)*
Energy from the Sun
www.fi.edu/PECO/sun-guide-family.pdf

Elements in the Sun - Solar Chemical Composition - Chemistry
chemistry.about.com

New role for the benefits of oxygen - Science Daily
www.sciencedaily.com/releases/2013/10/131004105238.htm

http://www.youtube.com/watch?v=oZgT1SRcrKE
Zeitgeist part 1 on Religion

Chapter IX: *The Heart's Sole (Sol) Purpose*
Web Page Title: Neurofeedback on the Brain: The Heart of Neurofeedback

Inside Article: The Heart of Neurofeedback

Sub-Article: What Happens When Our Hearts Are "Coherent"?
Written by Dr. Karen Shue
Published: 12/29/2005
Web link: www.neurofeedback.blogharbor.com

My Glossary

Being: *The Being* is the *conscious observer* and the conscious source of energy within a human being. Hence, *Being* is the most essential part of a human *being.* Therefore, *Being* here on this sacred planet and <u>*consciously*</u> experiencing other forms of life would be impossible without the nature of one's *Being*.

As human <u>Beings</u> our real reason for 'Being' is to <u>consciously</u> live life harmoniously; which can only be achieved through loving "All" forms of life.

Being Conscious: *Being conscious* is a reference that insinuates the following:

We as the *Being;* which lives within our human form is the *conscious* observer of life. Therefore, *'Being conscious'* of authentic life is extremely important to our overall well Being.

Consciousness: Consciousness as we currently perceive it is the state of being completely awake and aware.

However, in my opinion, consciousness is grasping the present moment with our *undivided attention* and fully experiencing it with all of our physical senses. Furthermore, the *true nature* of consciousness is more than just being aware of the present moment. Consciousness is the **<u>*'electromagnetic energy'*</u>** of this Universe that is concealed within the element that we call **<u>Oxygen</u>** and expresses itself in physical form. Consciousness is what defines and brings true meaning to life. Consciousness is a universal energy that is *perpetual* and *eternal*. Consciousness is the life, the light, and the truth that spark and manifest our reality.

Ego/Self: Our ego is a man-made representation of who we think we are. Our ego is what defines our man-made concept of *self.*

Our ego is who *we* work for; hence our ego is who bosses us around. Our ego rules and governs our reality; thus our ego is what totally controls our life. Our ego manipulates our thoughts and awareness and in turn makes all of our decisions.

Our ego ensures that we maintain and honor all of our *man-made beliefs.* Hence, *our ego is selfish,* which is why our *'ego'* and our *'self'* are considered to be one in the same.

God/Universe: ***This Universe is what defines the Power of Love!***

Now, allow me to take this moment to be crystal clear in regards to my idea of this Universe, as I address those who may struggle with their religious beliefs and find it impossible to believe that we are divine Beings, that are a reflection of this divine Universe.

When I refer to the divine nature of this Universe, I am not speaking to the <u>oppressive</u> and controlling subconscious notion that this Universe is an Omnipotent, Supernatural Ruler that we are not one with, so, therefore, we must obey Him or else *fear* 'His' wrath!

Hence, this *male* dictatorial version of this Universe has never presented him *'self'* in *real form,* which means 'He' is only the Ruler of our subconscious mind. Consequently this only supports a debilitating *make believe* concept that man him *'self'* has made us believe to be true.

Thus, when I speak of our *oneness* with this Universe, I am solely citing the <u>uplifting</u> essence of this Universe; whereas the divine energy of this Universe is what naturally defines our universal nature.

See, we human beings are all co-*creators **of*** this divine Universe. Therefore, as co-creators of this Universe we are naturally one with **'one'** Creator. Hence, I ask you what is 10% ***of*** 100? Well, regardless of what the answer is it is still a percentage ***of*** the <u>Whole</u>.

As co-creators of this divine Universe our mission is to collectively create the concept of Heaven on Earth; which can only be accomplished by way of living coherently through our universal nature —*which is the divine power of love!*

Human Avatar: The Human Avatar is a reference to our physical form; hence the *human form* or the *Human Avatar* is a *miraculous machine* that is controlled by one's consciousness. Thus, the more control we have of our consciousness, the more control we will have over this machine I call the *Human Avatar.*

Every Human Avatar comes equipped with a powerful *'self'* controlling mainframe; which we refer to as the human brain or the subconscious mind. This human brain is programmed by our sense of awareness and our thoughts.

Thus, this powerful component relies and responds only to our conscious input. And since we perceive our *'self'* as being our human forms; this *mistaken identity* has empowered our Human Avatar with the ability to control and manipulate our lives through a fraudulent perception.

Life: Life is the sacred energy of this Universe. Life is the intangible energy that fuels and brings every physical form to life. *Hence, there is "<u>no such thing as physical energy</u>"; considering the nature of energy is not physical.*

Life is holistic, life is pure, and life is static. Thus in reality; life is the *incorporeal conscious energy* that defines *'us' all.*

Love/Divinity: Love is the only *Universal feeling* that represents the real nature of every human being; and another name for love is *divinity.*

Thus, every human being is a *symbol of love* and it is only our beliefs that conceal our divinity.

Lying Beliefs: *Lying Beliefs* represent the questionable man-made beliefs that *lie deep* within the *reactive area* of our subconscious minds. These dubious beliefs are responsible for **under-minding** our behavior and forming our disturbing reality.

Man-Made Beliefs: What are man-made beliefs? Well, generally speaking all beliefs are man-made concepts and ideas that roam free within the *reactive* arena of our subconscious mind. It is only our *commanding* man-made beliefs that manifest our individual perception of life, as well as, rule our reality.

These man-made beliefs that lie festering within the reactive area of our subconscious mind are automatically stimulated based upon our awareness of certain scenarios and situations in life. Once our man-made beliefs are spontaneously activated, this is what forms our man-made behavior, which is also called our *second nature*. Or better yet; should I say our *worst nature!*

Pursuit of Wholeness: The Pursuit of Wholeness is becoming aware of our universal nature. The Pursuit of Wholeness is the process of ultimately realizing that our human form bears no resemblance to who we really are.

The Pursuit of Wholeness is coming to the *conscious conclusion* that the Sol or Sun of this Universe lives within us and it is only this sacred "*Wholly light*" that defines the soul of who we are.

Sole/Soul: The dual words of *sole/soul* represent a dual meaning whereas; *The Universe's 'Sol/Soul' is the one and only electro-magnetic energy that 'solely' defines us.*

Subconscious Beliefs: Subconscious beliefs are man-made beliefs that lie deep within our subconscious minds; which in turn support our paradigms. Subconscious beliefs are man-made beliefs that we human beings live by, which ultimately become a part of our *second nature*; because we do not think to grant these suspicious beliefs a *second thought*. Thus in truth, there is no such thing as a *'conscious' belief.*

Every man-made belief that we live by resides only within our *'subconscious' mind.*

Subconscious Emotions: Subconscious emotions are byproducts of our unawareness that habitually dwells upon the man-made madness that *molds* our subconscious mind. Hence, how we *feel* is contingent upon what we human beings *'subconsciously' or incoherently think* about the most.

Thus, we human beings spend our entire lives, via our *unawareness*, inside our subconscious mind *thinking* upon man's version of *Self, Life, and God*, which is why we *worry about man's concept of life, fear* the man-made idea of this Universe, and are extremely *'Self' conscious*.

Although love is the natural emotion that defines our true nature, we human beings seldom have thoughts of love. And because we ignore our divine nature and choose to think upon the man-made stigma that occupies our subconscious mind; we unfortunately experience man-made or *'subconscious emotions' of fear, worry, hate, depression, etc.*

Subconscious Mind: From my perspective, the subconscious mind is comprised of the following three levels: Analytical, Creative, and **Reactive** and it's the *Reactive level* that is crucial to the survival of us human beings. The Reactive level is where our beliefs reside. Thus, our behavior, as well as our perception is primarily determined from this level, as it relates to how we human beings *spontaneously* **react** towards life.

The subconscious mind is the most powerful gift <u>unknown</u> to humanity. Thus, the subconscious mind can either be a *blessing* or a *curse* to us human beings.

The subconscious mind is connected to this Almighty Universe.

The subconscious mind is all-knowing and *'self'* controlling. Hence, in this *Whole Universe* there is only *'one universal mind'*, and that is the subconscious mind. This means the so called *conscious mind* is merely a *presumed mind.* Considering, a conscious mind or any other mind for that *matter*, has yet to be discovered.

The subconscious mind is responsible for aiding in the development and manifestation of our beliefs. The subconscious mind stores our memories; in other words *registers our conscious experiences*.

The subconscious mind adheres to our thoughts and our awareness. The subconscious mind honors our desires, as well as our *fears and worries*. The subconscious mind is what ensures that *"we get what we give."* Hence, whatever we *religiously believe in* or think about the most our subconscious mind will do whatever is necessary to bring our beliefs to fruition, even if the fruition is in the *form of an illusion.*

Our subconscious mind can either be *our companion* or *our enemy.* And the only way our subconscious mind can ever be our companion is if we do not rely on it to define who we are. However, our subconscious mind will forever be our enemy, as long as we refer to the *man-made concepts* that reside within our subconscious mind for our *'self'* identity.

Hence, the current state of our subconscious mind can also be referred to as the **Man-Made Mind.** Considering, as it stands now, our subconscious mind is controlling us solely based upon our *man-made beliefs.*

Subconscious Thoughts: Subconscious thoughts are thoughts that we human beings are producing unknowingly. And these thoughts that we are totally unaware of, are based upon the man-made propaganda that is stored within our subconscious minds.

Hence, these subconscious thoughts are formulated from dwelling upon the man-made ideas, concepts, theories, beliefs, etc., that lurk deep within our subconscious mind.

Universal Sol/Sun: The *Sol/Sun* of this Universe is the *'Wholly'* beacon of enlightenment that *shines* ITS *conscious love* down upon us. The *Sol/Sun* of this Universe is the *sacred light* that shines within the physical form of every living Being and bestows upon us *consciousness, life, and love.*

Hence, it is the *Sol/Sun* of this Universe that fills our Solar System with the *spiritual energy that we call air; which grants us all conscious life* and is why we are considered to be *living sols/souls.*

You/Soul/Spirit: *You are the conscious **soul**, You are the **soul observer**, You are the solar **spirit** of this Universe!*

Thus, you are *bodiless* and *intangible*. Hence, you are *untouchable*. Meaning you are the *consciousness*; you are the *miracle of life;* you are the *thinker;* and you are the *awareness.*

You are indeed the *'spiritual light'* or the Sun of this Universe. You are the divine *'Being'* that manifest itself through your human form or through your Human Avatar.

You represent all the *unseen mystical phenomenons* in this divine Universe; which makes you a *phenomenal human being*. And last but not least; you are the *'immortal spiritual conscious energy'* of this divine Universe that we human beings refer to as God!

PROFESSIONAL BOOK REVIEWS

"Lying Beliefs by Maurice Johnson is a book about a very unique perspective on life and how we see ourselves. The writing style is simple, engaging, and the book is written in an informal, conversational tone that creates an easy connection with readers. A book from a unique perspective and one that I would recommend to all!" —*Readers' Favorite, Five Star Review*

"This is a multi-faceted book embracing a broad spectrum of subject matters. Here, the author unravels religious, spiritual, and scientific components in an effort to question the man-made beliefs that undermine our behavior, creating what he claims to be our false sense of self. Stressing that we are all born pure in body, mind, and soul, he counterpoints that our wealth and material obsessions will lead us down a path toward spiritual bankruptcy. Johnson's discussions run the gamut from Freudian levels of awareness, to believing Jesus was an enlightened human being, to modern scientific research. His book serves as a guide to help readers through the perplexed quagmire.

Interleaving Christian religious beliefs comparatively to modern science, the author uses the model that oxygen is synonymous with consciousness. Considering oxygen and hydrogen are primary elements of the human body, and also two of the most essential components of the Sun, Johnson offers the Sun's essence as representing the light defining each of our souls. A strong emphasis is placed on the importance of mindfulness being in the present; clearly a concept reflective of *Buddhist* traditions. Dwelling on the past or an imaginary future will only consume us with worry and negativity. There is an interesting correlation to man's best friend – dogs – noting with their instinctive awareness, dogs live in the present, have no ego, and maintain a soulful relationship with man. Johnson also considers the dog/GOD anadrome reflective of a dog's soul touching the human heart.

In his lighter vein, readers get a momentary reprieve from the comparative style format of his narrative, as Johnson infuses his writing with poetic verse. *The True Mystery of Life* speaks of this enigma as our soul energy, while another poem about the sunset seems reflective of the commentary about spiritual essence linking our conscious energy emanating from the "One Sun."

Johnson cleverly sets his writing within a contemporary framework, referencing icons of pop culture and entertainment. Here he modifies renowned self-help guru Dr. Wayne Dyer's acronym for EGO, and notes the irony in singer John Mayer's composition *Waiting on the World to Change*. "We," he advises are the ones needing refinement, not the world outside. Likening our physical form to a "Human Avatar," Johnson highlights the film's revealing of the inner soul's defining of our true nature. Stated is the author's concurrence, "There is far more to us than meets the physical eye."

Covering such varied and intricate thematic landscapes, this is a truly inspirational and contemplative read. With its reference to "Knowledge is Power," Johnson offers just such an advantage for those seeking the deeper truth of soul enrichment of fundamental enlightenment." **—Pacific Book Review, Five Star Review**

PACIFIC BOOK REVIEW INTERVIEW

PBR:

Your spiritual writing seems to indicate some Buddhist influences and those ideas about connection and "wholeness" seem to indicate people being interconnected. Was this informed by ideas such as global or cultural 'Jung' consciousness?

Maurice:

As far back as I can remember I have always been in pursuit of a better sense of what actually defines me. Therefore, I would only feast off of information that fed and nurtured my true essence. And the variety of information I selectively digested was not limited to any specific genre, concept, or idea.

I would have to say that I am more of an enigma; considering I am not an avid reader and I've never had aspirations to become a writer. I was 'inspired' to write solely based upon a deeper sense of knowing what truly defines me.

And as many of us live our lives in pursuit of academic degree(s) in order to achieve a higher level of learning; I on the other hand, have simply been in the pursuit of obtaining a higher degree of *knowing*.

In my opinion the spiritual Buddhist teachings regarding the laws of nature, as well as the *conscious teachings of Jesus*, are indicative of two human beings who were highly enlightened. And both of their messages are interconnected and serve as a platform to seek *'wholeness'* through *enlightenment*.

As it pertains specifically to Jesus, from my perspective he was a *light messenger.* His mission was to have us all pursue *wholeness* through understanding that beyond what we physically see we are all interconnected by way of one illuminating *solar light of conscious energy*—which makes us all the *light of this world.*

Regardless of how one defines enlightenment, it is certainly not an overnight sensation, it is a journey. Thus, in order for one to become truly enlightened, you must possess the courage to look beyond what you have been conditioned to believe. And as you travel through this intricate puzzle we call life, you must innately sense via feelings of congruency, what pieces of wisdom are actually fitting to your internal exploration. Then, when you least expect it, you may stumble upon that final piece *peace* of wisdom that will complete your puzzling life. Only then will the true meaning of life and love come together. Hence, this beautiful experience will become the final conclusion to your pursuit of wholeness.

PBR:

Given your critique of the self or ego; do you think the historical characterizations of God as an individual (usually a He) have actually been harmful and led to selfish behavior?

Maurice:

This is a very fascinating question. Although, before I directly respond to this question, allow me to first say that the word *'God'* is nothing more than a man-made name that is used to define a powerful *unseen* force of *conscious 'electromagnetic'* energy that stems from this Universe. And historically man has been known to portray this mystical energy in **'His'** own image.

When you confine such a sacred energy into the image of one individual, you diminish the *vast* nature of this divine Universe, which can result in a selfish and harmful behavior.

When we worship this Universe as being a man or in the *form* of any *individual image,* we are only worshipping a cultural concept that has been *formed* by man. Each culture around the world bears its own man-made concept of this Universe and these concepts are respectively ingrained within the psyche of each respective member.

These members are coerced into praising and worshipping only their cultural concept of this Universe as being their one and only true Redeemer. Based upon this tremendous misconception of our *universal* nature; we human beings tend to develop a *self-destructive behavior* towards those who oppose our conditioned concept of who we subconsciously think this Universe is. Since, we human beings fail to comprehend the mechanics of our subconscious mind; we are persuaded to live a mechanical life. And because we have never been informed on how to operate and control our subconscious minds we unknowingly allow ourselves to be manipulated by our own minds.

Whether we recognize this or not, the power of prayer is not based upon the man-made God(s) that we have been deceived to believe in. The power of prayer is simply contingent upon the bona fide fact that **we believe!**

In other words, it is only our divine energy and the degree of *our faith* that fuels *our beliefs*. Therefore, it is this process in itself that truly spawns—and is responsible—for our prayers being answered. Thus the cultural God(s) that we have been trained to worship via prayer is nothing more than a figment of our man-made imagination. In conscious reality, there is no form of any man-made idea of this Universe that is actually basking in the clouds and taking our lives into consideration through *individually* honoring our prayers.

However, since the majority of humanity believes that the God(s) that we have been conditioned to worship are indeed responsible for addressing our prayers; this deception will forever force us to fear and worship a false concept of this Universe's true shining aura. Unfortunately, this diminishes our true nature to love another human being as we would love ourselves, because we have *selfishly* relinquished all of our love, to a selfish man-made version of this Universe.

In truth, this Universe can never be defined as a physical or material image, because the true nature of this Universe is the *formless* essence of *love*. And love is the one and only sacred emotion that defines us all. If we take the time to consciously think about it, there is actually nothing physical or material about love. However, what I do find intriguing is that love is something that you don't have to *touch* in order to *feel*.

PBR:

This book has a religious (no, spiritual) basis, and it seems to encourage the individual to be self-reliant, consciously aware, and in charge of his or her actions. Are you arguing that a person should have faith in his/herself rather than in some notion of a God-self?

Maurice:

This is another great question; however please allow me to be crystal clear in terms of my '*self*' perspective. Quite frankly, the *self* that I am referring to has yet to be introduced to the subconscious mind of humanity. And the *self* that I am referring to is indeed the notion of a *God-Self or Universal-Self*, versus the concept of a *Man-Made-Self*; which today is the *self* that most of humanity complies with; which depicts a fraudulent concept of who we truly are.

Please allow me to elaborate. The book actually speaks of encouraging individuals to do some real *soul* searching in order to discover that the *Sol* or the *Sun* of this Universe lives within them. This way they can be freed from their man-made sense of self.

In other words, this book aims to distinguish the astonishing difference between our *immortal universal-self,* which ultimately defines us, versus our man-made self that secretly undermines us.

Hence, as it stands now our disturbing behavior is based upon a man-made concept of our self, which is currently in charge of our lives. Our false perception of self also makes us take subconscious actions based upon man-made concepts that we have been conditioned to value and vindicate.

If we take a step back and analyze our sense of self we will notice that our human self-possesses a multitude of different identities, all of which combines to define us.

Please keep me honest, but from my vantage point, it seems as if our self is only defined by the suspicious data outlined within our subconscious mind. Unfortunately, we have misconstrued our conscious encounters that reside within our subconscious warehouse as what naturally defines us versus viewing this data as nothing more than information that defines the nature of our overall conscious experiences.

Thus, from our perception, we use the following man-made concepts to define our man-made self: *Nationality, Culture, Race, Ethnicity, Religion, Political affiliation, etc.,* and as long as these *selfish* notions of who we think we are continue to rule our reality our universal *'God-Self'* will forever remain a secret. Therefore, the last thing we human beings should be is *self-reliant* upon our man-made sense of *self.*

From my viewpoint the perception that we have of our selves initially stems from what we physically see in the mirror. And based upon our human reflection, there are man-made concepts that are associated with our man-made self that we all robotically oblige and obey. This means it is literally these man-made conflicting concepts that we individually uphold and live by that actually divides us because, we have been thoroughly conditioned to believe that these man-made concepts personify us.

Therefore, the true purpose of this book is to make a valid attempt to have us human beings shift our conscious awareness from our *'destructive' man-made sense of self,* towards a more *'constructive' Universal essence of self*; in order to become more unified and harmonious human beings.

If we really look beyond our paradigms, we will instinctively realize how our physical form that we believe represents us, actually bears no relevance, as to who we truly are. Without the formless phenomenon(s) of *consciousness, thought, and life* there can never be a physical sense of self.

Therefore, we human beings need to shift our self-awareness to become more aware that we all share the *Immortal Sol of One Universe* which will then allow our consciousness to rise and shine within our subconscious mind which will in turn lay our distressed Man-Made-Self down to rest.

See, the *conscious energy of formless life or the spiritual energy of this Universe* is what exists within all physical forms of nature and is what motivates the expression *"God is everywhere."* Hence, all living forms of nature are simply the consciousness of this Universe experiencing unique spirited forms of *itself*. We human beings are a more *sophisticated form* of this Universe's consciousness, considering our divinity is defined by the magnitude of our conscious capacity to exude the energy of universal Love!

PBR:

You talk about the "heart brain" which I had never heard of before. This is an interesting theory especially considering the historical connections between the heart and emotions. Can you elaborate on this idea (brain in the heart) as it applies on a spiritual level?

Maurice:

The brain in the heart theory is based upon research performed by the folks at HeartMath; which revealed the heart is an organ that is more complex than we may have previously thought, based upon a specialized set of neurons discovered within the human heart.

And it is these *'sensory'* neurons, based upon our level of conscious awareness that communicates information to our *Solar* plexus; which in turn creates what we commonly refer to as a *gut-feeling.*

However, addressing the heart from a more spiritual perspective, the human heart is primarily designed to bestow upon the human form feelings of love and joy, which are feelings that are in direct harmony with our divine nature.

Although, in this seemingly devilish world that we *subconsciously* dwell in, it is virtually impossible for us human beings not to experience feelings that conflict with our true emotional nature.

I sense it is safe to say that our attention determines how we feel emotionally.

Hence, although our heart is principally created to makes us feel divine, our heart can only bestow upon us glorious feelings, if we essentially do our part, by showering it with pleasurable and delightful thoughts. Because we fail to live coherently through the loving chambers of our heart, this incoherent disconnection from the essence of love, steers our attention towards our brain, which is a domain that is mainly filled with harmful and detrimental information.

And since we spend the majority of our life perched upon questionable man-made concepts and beliefs that reside within our subconscious mind, this misuse of our attention and our thoughts tend to influence our heart to stimulate our human form with the man-made emotions of *fear, hate, worry, and despair.*

Whether we grasp the following concept or not, our feelings are the foundation to our reality. Which means it is safe to say that in reality, all we really want out of life is to feel loved! Therefore, we must stay in tune with our loving heart.

PBR:

I am always interested in language and thought. You note a number of linguistic similarities and puns—i.e., soul, sole, solar—which illustrate connections between physical and spiritual energy. This is sort of a chicken and the egg question. Do you think these linguistic connections were divinely inspired, a fortuitous accident in the development of languages, etc.?

Maurice:

This is a fantastic question! Well, from my perspective El *Sol* or the *Sun of this Universe* has been revered by man long before modern day religion. And with El Sol being the *sole* source of *solar* energy, it appears that the linguistic connection of *soul* and *solar* both stem from one *sole* source of electromagnetic energy called *El Sol*.

Now, in regards to language and the number of puns and other similarities that I reference throughout the book, especially as it relates to spiritual energy, I also speak of consciousness as being a synonym for oxygen. And because this is an idea that has never been introduced to the paradigms of humanity, I do realize that some individuals may view my perspective of El Sol as being the bearer of consciousness as an irregular and questionable theory.

Well, what I would like to explain to those skeptics is that until a supposed conscious mind is unveiled, all I ask is that you try to envision the rationale behind my conscious theory. This theory suggests that we *do not have a conscious mind*, because the electro-magnetic energy from Universe's *Sol* is what creates our consciousness.

I am sure that most of humanity is familiar with the expression "*Mind, Body, and Soul/Sol.*" Well, do you also notice how all three of these entities stand alone and most importantly do you realize that the *'Mind'* is not plural? In my opinion this means we only have *one mind!*

Therefore, it appears as if this *sole mind* can only be associated with our *subconscious mind*; considering the existence of a conscious mind has yet to be discovered.

This means consciousness can only be defined by either the soul *sol* or the human body. And, based upon the process of elimination, the notion that our body alone exudes consciousness should not even be considered a factor. Therefore, this leaves us with only one *sole solution* and that is the soul *sol* of who we are is what truly represents our consciousness.

Please allow me to elaborate, every physical form of life breathes. And every breath that we consume is *solar energy*. Hence, it is only the Sun of this Universe that bestows *conscious life* within every physical form of life.

Although some of us may be under the notion that the Sun is only responsible for our *physical* existence, what we must discern is that the sacred nature of life is **not** physical.

<u>*In other words, our physical form does not produce the miracle of conscious life; it is our miraculous life that manifests itself through our physical form.*</u>

Therefore, we human beings need to reverse our way of thinking and acknowledge that our human form which we have been conditioned to believe exemplifies us, does not possess a soul. However, it is indeed the soul *Sol* of this Universe, which truly defines us; that actually has ownership of a human form.

My theory in terms of consciousness is based upon actual reality. Every physical form of life requires *oxygen* in order to *consciously* survive; thus my innate theory in regards to oxygen being nothing more than a scientific or technical term for consciousness. Therefore in my opinion; *life* and *consciousness* are completely contingent upon one another. Hence, it is only our consciousness that allows us to physically feel and experience other forms of life.

Based upon every single breath we take; solar energy is relayed to our heart, and in conjunction with our oxygen *(conscious)* enriched blood; the solar energy of conscious life is distributed throughout every aspect of our human body and of course including our brain. And it is this conscious energy that makes us all *living souls 'sols'*, which consciously experience life through a human form.

I notice in the question you reference the notion of *physical energy*. However, in reality, there is no physical or material object that possesses the capability to produce energy on its own. Energy is not a physical object. It's only the spiritual energy of conscious life that animates an inanimate object.

Therefore, the connection between our physical body and *spiritual energy* is based upon an interconnection, whereas the Universe's spiritual conscious energy that enters into the human form, via the air we breathe, is what grants our physical body the *conscious energy of life*. Hence, in the absence of spiritual or solar energy, there can never be a lively physical presence, considering, the conscious energy of life, which is *formless*, is what generates our physical existence.

Our Earth orbits within a vast Solar System where 99.86% of our Solar System's mass is occupied by God's Immortal Sol. Every living Being that consciously resides on Planet Earth *solely* exists through the divine air we breathe. And because we all share the same sacred air, we are all *interconnected* and adjoined to the same loving family. Considering through every breath we take, we are all *Heirs 'airs'* of the Universe's one and only *Sun*.

And it is the Universe's Sun that *religiously* rises or resurrects every morning, in order to *faithfully* shine down upon us life and unconditional love. Hence the Sun of this Universe is the *true light of this world* that cast out the darkness and provides humanity with a bright tomorrow.

What I find interesting is we human beings are extremely loyal to our conditioned beliefs; i.e., since we have been conditioned to believe that the air we breathe is called *oxygen* it's difficult for us to fathom that this divine air that grants us our *conscious existence* can be referred to as anything else.

Well, in terms of language isn't oxygen just another man-made word? Therefore, couldn't consciousness, which is another man-made word that has yet to be explained, simply be another name to describe the divine air we breathe?

The first step towards enlightenment is to realize that our lives are essentially managed by the language of man-made concepts that should be debated. And if we never argue the linguistic concepts that we live by, then we will always be compelled to question our life's purpose.

About the Author

I am a humble soul who was born in Buffalo, NY on April 26, 1965 and I have been married to the same lovely woman for approximately 18 years. We have been blessed to share our lives with beautiful twin boys who fill our lives with joy.

I am not associated with any religion. However, despite my lack of involvement with any religious doctrine I have always had a tremendous *sense* of someone or more so *'something'* within me.

As far back as I can remember I have always been in pursuit of a better sense of what defines me. Therefore, I would only feast off of information that fed and nurtured my true essence. *And the variety of information I selectively digested was not limited to any specific genre, concept, or idea.*

I would have to say that I am more of an enigma considering I am not an avid reader and I've never had aspirations to become a writer. Hence, I was *inspired* to write, solely based upon a deeper sense of knowing what truly defines me. And as many of us live our lives in pursuit of academic degrees in order to achieve a higher level of learning, I on the other hand, have simply been in the pursuit of obtaining a higher degree of *knowing*.

Maurice Johnson
Author and New World Philosopher

About the Author

Then on February 6, 2012, I plugged into the sacred truth in terms of what *naturally* defines me and on this date I uncovered that my *man-made sense of self* is a false representation of who I truly am.

Therefore, my sole/*soul* goal is to share my conscious experience with humanity—with the intention of freeing as many of my sibling souls as I possibly can from their man-made sense of self. I consider it is primarily our conditioned man-made perception of who we *think* we are that is responsible for our human suffering.

NEXT STEPS

Universal Call To Action

We all need to understand that this Universe is desperately trying to get in touch with us; however it seems as if we are disconnected from the line of communication that stems from this Universe; which means our <u>awareness seems to be out of service</u>.

We human beings are so busy conversing with our egos that we have placed this *'urgent'* call to action from the Universe on hold.

<u>Here is my call to action:</u>

The creation of *Lying Beliefs* answers my *initial* call to action. However, I have come to know that this Universe will always "call upon me" to do what is right for my fellow human being; therefore my life's mission is to assist with shifting my fellow soul's awareness towards their divinity. I am inspired towards re-cultivating the current scenery of the human psyche in order to improve the spiritual landscape of our world. My motivation is based upon helping us all become better human beings through discovering what better defines us.

Okay, I have shared with you my call to action, now I ask you; *"<u>What's Yours!</u>"*

If you are someone who, deep down inside, 'knows' that this world does not accurately reflect the way 'life' should be, and if you realize the chaos which infects this world is a direct result of us human beings defending our *beliefs*, and if you also sense the antidote for "World Peace" can only be remedied through injecting more *'Love into this world'*; then you must venture deep down into the soul of who you are and do what is necessary to reverse your form of thinking in order to assist with creating the concept of Heaven on Earth; before the concept of 'HELL' becomes our _everlasting_ reality.

If you *'felt'* that the information communicated in *Lying Beliefs* was useful and it has inspired a movement within you; then please by all means use this *literary inspiration* to infuse others. Please know we should not be *'selfish'* with enlightenment. In other words, inspiration should not be 'self' contained, it should be unleashed to inspire others to achieve their own personal **call to action**!

Further Enlightenment

If the information conveyed in this book expanded your awareness and has in turn *"Stretched the boundaries on your path to enlightenment"* by way of shining light on the truths you have been seeking, then I have fulfilled my initial call to action.

However, if you have any comments, questions, or concerns, by all means, please feel free to contact me at:

Website: www.lyingbeliefs.com
Email: maurice@nomoego.com

www.ingramcontent.com/pod-product-compliance
Lightning Source LLC
Chambersburg PA
CBHW071945110426
42744CB00030B/292